SAMS
Teach Yourself

MICROSOFT® SQL
SERVER™ 7

William Robison

in 10 Minutes

D1057291

SAMS

A Division of Macmillan Computer Publishing
201 West 103rd St., Indianapolis, Indiana, 46290 USA

Sams Teach Yourself Microsoft® SQL Server™ 7 in 10 Minutes

Copyright © 1999 by Sams Publishing

International Standard Book Number: 0-672-31663-3

Library of Congress Catalog Card Number: 99-61494

Printed in the United States of America

First Printing: August 1999

01   00   4   3   2

Trademarks

Warning and Disclaimer

ASSOCIATE PUBLISHER
Bradley L. Jones

AQUISITIONS EDITOR
Sharon Cox

DEVELOPMENT EDITOR
Thomas Cirtin

TECHNICAL EDITOR
Ivan Oss

MANAGING EDITOR
Jodi Jensen

SENIOR EDITOR
Susan Ross Moore

COPY EDITOR
Linda Morris

INDEXER
Christine Nelsen

PROOFREADER
Megan Wade

TEAM COORDINATOR
Meggo Barthlow

INTERIOR DESIGN
Gary Adair

COVER DESIGN
Aren Howell

COPY WRITER
Eric Borgert

LAYOUT TECHNICIANS
Darin Crone
Liz Johnston

Contents

About the Author

William Robison, a Microsoft Certified Systems Engineer and Technical Lead with TRW, Inc. in Fairfax, VA, has more than ten years' experience in application, server, and complete system design and development. His professional experience includes a range of architectural, design, and programming tasks on platforms from desktop PCs and Windows NT and UNIX servers to IBM mainframe applications. To this work he brings over five years' experience with RDBMS applications, including ODBC programming to SQL Server from version 4.3 through version 7.0. Mr. Robison's professional interests include physical modeling, simulation, and visualization.

Dedication

To my sons, Marc and Nicholas.

Acknowledgments

The people who have contributed to everything I do are too numerous to name. Once upon a time, my father built a homebrew computer instead of buying me an Intellivision; instead of packaged game cartridges, I had to write my own games on a half-stock, half-grown Polymorphics Poly-88. Though not at the time, it's apparent now where a fascinating and exciting career began.

To bring this particular work to fruition, I have to point to Neil Rowe, who got me started; Sharon Cox, who kept it all together and going forward; and Tom Cirtin, who tried to keep my foot out of my mouth. Special thanks go to Ivan Oss, whose knowledge and attention to detail made a huge difference. The many others who have worked with me at Macmillan know my gratefulness, I hope, even if I can't list them all.

Most important of all are family and friends who have encouraged me, checked in on me, and put up with me: Brandi, Marc, Nicky, the Jerrys, Jeff, Roger, Tayyaba, Anita, and the incredible Rita. You have my thanks. Whenever I run out of ideas, you always have more for me.

Tell Us What You Think!

As the reader of this book, *you* are our most important critic and commentator. We value your opinion and want to know what we're doing right, what we could do better, what areas you'd like to see us publish in, and any other words of wisdom you're willing to pass our way.

As an Associate Publisher for Sams Publishing, I welcome your comments. You can fax, email, or write me directly to let me know what you did or didn't like about this book—as well as what we can do to make our books stronger.

Please note that I cannot help you with technical problems related to the topic of this book, and that due to the high volume of mail I receive, I might not be able to reply to every message.

When you write, please be sure to include this book's title and author as well as your name and phone or fax number. I will carefully review your comments and share them with the author and editors who worked on the book.

Fax: 317-581-4770

Email: adv_prog@mcp.com

Mail: Bradley L. Jones
          Associate Publisher
          Sams Publishing
          201 West 103rd Street
          Indianapolis, IN 46290 USA

Introduction

Welcome to SQL Server 7! This book will teach you about one of the most feature-laden database servers on the market. Although many books have described this rich relational database management system in exhaustive detail, there's a distinct lack of help in just getting up to speed and becoming productive quickly. This book addresses that particular problem: I assume you don't need to know everything about how SQL Server works, you just need to get your job done. With this book, you will gain a sound basis for powerful problem-solving with SQL Server.

The book is arranged into three main parts:

- In Lessons 1–4, you'll learn the basics of what a relational database is and how to retrieve and modify data.

- In Lessons 5–10, you'll see how to put the database to work using data in popular applications like Microsoft's Word and Excel, and how to publish data to a Web site.

- Lessons 11–20 take you further into SQL Server, showing you how to build databases, analyze data, perform basic administration tasks, and move and transform data.

Even if you already "know SQL Server," take a look inside. This book, which goes beyond a tutorial, represents one of the most concise distillations of common SQL Server tasks you will find, and presents its information in a task-oriented form that makes it quite handy as a reference. I plan to keep a copy on my desk. You may find it has a place on yours.

Conventions Used in This Book

To help you move through the lessons easily, the following icons are used:

 Plain English   New or unfamiliar terms are defined in (you got it) "plain English."

Note Notes provide additional information that is tangential, yet relevant, to the topic at hand.

Tip Look here for ideas that cut corners and confusion.

Caution This icon identifies areas where new users often run into trouble, and it offers practical solutions to those problems.

LESSON 1
What Is SQL Server?

In this lesson, you'll learn the overall structure of SQL Server 7 and the services it provides you.

SQL Server is a relational database management system, or RDBMS. An RDBMS stores data in a structured form on a database *server*, allowing many people to use the data from other computers, termed *clients*, at one time. This lesson will give you a general overview of what SQL Server is and how it does its job.

SQL Server Components

SQL Server 7 is composed of several services running on Windows NT/Windows 2000 or background programs on Windows 98. These services are MSSQLServer (SQL Server), the Search Service, MSDTC, and SQLServerAgent. The services are illustrated graphically in Figure 1.1. Another service you might hear of is the OLAP Service, which is outside the scope of this book.

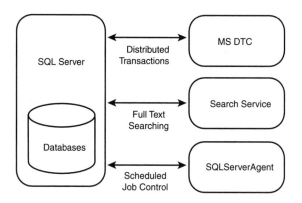

FIGURE 1.1   SQL Server Services.

The SQL Server service is the core database manager and is the only service that *must* be running. The distributed transaction coordinator (MSDTC) interacts with other SQL Servers and with MS Transaction Server (MTS) to coordinate transactions with applications that run on more than one computer or technology. The Search service handles full text searching, enabling you to search through textual data in your database; the Search service is not installed by default, so it may not be present on your server. Finally, SQLServerAgent is a task scheduler that handles all periodic tasks, such as maintenance and replication.

These processes work together to manage and give you access to databases. A SQL Server can host many databases on the same server. Every SQL Server will have at least the model, msdb, master, and tempdb databases. You will usually find two sample databases, Northwind and pubs, as well as your business's databases. Multiple databases enable different business areas to be grouped into independent entities to simplify management without requiring multiple server instances to serve users.

As you work with SQL Server, you will discover it has capabilities that need one or more of the peripheral processes to be running. For example, if you want to run scheduled tasks, you'll need SQLServerAgent running on the server. If you are a user of the system (not an administrator), you will have to coordinate with the administrator for any services you need that aren't already available.

Tip   Without a doubt, you will have questions as you use SQL Server. For answers, try Books Online. Books Online is a comprehensive set of manuals that describes every aspect of SQL Server, from administration to obscure methods of programming applications. Books Online also contains an index and a full-text search facility, whereby you can find any information you need in the books. Because it is distributed as a compiled HTML (.chm) file, you can download the manual set to your client workstation for faster access and searches.

Database Elements

A relational database stores and manipulates much more than just data. Before you get into the details of SQL Server, let's take a high-level look at the pieces you will see in a relational database.

Objects

Most things in the database itself are *objects*. The following paragraphs introduce the most common ones. These objects are all *persistent*; that is, they are stored in the database and don't go away when you log out or when the server shuts down.

A *table* is the basic data structure of a database. All information in the database is stored in tables, in a row/column layout that makes it easy to manipulate the data. In a table, each row is a *record* of data, and the columns are the *fields* of the record. Tables are explored in detail in Lesson 2, "Understanding Databases."

An *index* is similar to the index in a book, but instead of helping you find a topic, it helps the database server find a row of data in the table. When you ask for rows with particular column values, SQL Server looks for an index that can help locate those rows before it goes looking through all the data in the table. If there is no index, SQL Server must scan all the rows in the table, just as you would have to scan through a book with no index. Indices are explored in detail in Lesson 2.

A *view* can be thought of as a permanent, predefined retrieval from the database. If you have a set of information you commonly need to look for in the database, you can create a view to hold the command to retrieve the data. With a view, you don't need to retype the command every time you need the data; better still, others can use the view to see the data, too. This can be a real timesaver, especially if the command to retrieve the data is complex or retrieves data from many different tables. Views are discussed in Lesson 16, "Simplifying Common Queries."

A *constraint* is an object that defines a restriction on how or what kind of data can be stored in the database, with the intent of keeping the data *consistent*, or realistic. For example, an inventory table might place a NOT NULL constraint on the column holding the quantity on hand. Constraints are discussed in Lesson 2.

Consistent   A database is consistent if all the data in it agree with each other and the database's design. Storing a part number in an inventory table that didn't match a part in a parts definition table or storing a negative number for a person's age are two examples of inconsistent data.

A *stored procedure* is similar to a view because it stores SQL commands in the database, but a stored procedure can execute any SQL command (not just a retrieval), and can take parameters, such as retrieval criteria, that modify its operation each time you execute it. Stored procedures are discussed in Lesson 14, "Storing SQL in the Database."

A *trigger* can be thought of as a special kind of stored procedure. Triggers are attached to tables in the database and can be executed any time data is added, modified, or deleted from the table. Triggers are discussed in Lesson 15, "Controlling How Changes Are Made."

A *default* is a value that SQL Server will supply for a column if you add a row to a table and don't fill in that column.

A *user-defined data type (UDT)* is a specific definition of the kind of data that can go in a column. SQL Server supplies standard types that can handle numbers and textual data. You can use UDTs to define data more specifically than you can with the built-in data types. However, they can be problematic and are beyond the scope of this book.

Relations

A database that stores only tables is useful, to be sure. The most popular PC database of the 1980's, Ashton-Tate's dBASE, was a table-only database, often called a *flat-file* database. You can accomplish a lot with just this simple method of organization, but SQL Server and other RDBMSs add significant capability by enabling you to associate rows in different tables using a concept called a *relation*.

With a flat-file database, data almost always need to be associated from different files, but the operation has to be done in user code using the database manager's proprietary language. In relational databases, these relations are

A table, in SQL terms, is composed of columns and rows. Each row in the table stores information for one entity or relation (see Figure 2.1). Columns are the fields in each row that contain the attributes of each entity.

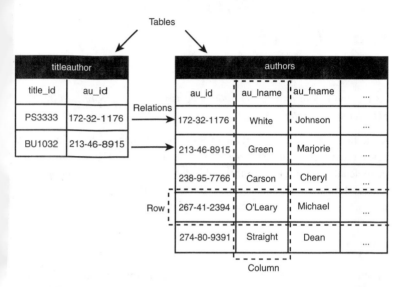

FIGURE 2.1 Database building blocks.

A table should have a set of data, ideally only a single column, that uniquely identifies each individual row in the table. For example, because the government assures that each person's Social Security Account Number (SSAN) is unique, the authors table in pubs uses it as the au_id to uniquely identify the authors.

In database terms, the row identifier is called the *primary key* and is required for most relations. Because the primary key value is used to identify the row and will be reproduced in any index or table that references it, you should choose the smallest reasonable data type that will accurately identify rows in the table.

Columns

Columns store the individual pieces of data in a row of a table. Columns have two main characteristics: their size and type. You will usually not be concerned with the size of the column, with one exception: You cannot

stored in the database itself. Almost no table you will work with contains data that is unrelated to any other data, so by handling these relations explicitly, it is easier both to create and to maintain a reliable, consistent database.

As a very simple example, consider the employee and jobs tables in the pubs database. Each job in the jobs table is identified by a unique job_id. Each employee in employee is *related* to a job by a job_id that is part of the employee record. This relation has to exist; if you had an employee without a job, it wouldn't make much sense.

Queries

A query is a command that you send to SQL Server through a database client program. You write these commands using the *lingua franca* of relational databases: the Structured Query Language (SQL). Every SQL command is referred to as a *query*, even though many commands don't retrieve anything (as you might expect from something called a *query*). Since nearly all modern database servers use SQL as their query language, you'll be able to use much of the SQL and database techniques in this books with other database servers, too.

Everything you do with SQL Server becomes a query at some point, though you might not actually see the query itself. You might be clicking buttons and check boxes in a graphical user interface (GUI), but the application responds to your commands by sending a query to the database behind the scenes, as shown in Figure 1.2.

Query commands can be grouped into three major categories:

- *Data definition language (DDL)*: DDL refers to the set of SQL statements you use in queries to define objects such as tables, constraints, stored procedures, and views. DDL is used to create the persistent structure and features of your database.

- *Data manipulation language (DML)*: DML, the subset of SQL you will use most of the time, is the group of statements such as SELECT and INSERT that you use to retrieve, analyze, modify, or delete data in your database. The DML statements are conceptually very simple, but they are incredibly powerful tools for working with information.

- *Data control language (DCL)*: DCL is used to define access controls on your data. As a user interacts with the database, the database server checks the user's permissions and grants or denies access to data and functions based on rules set by the administrator or the owner of the data. DCL is used to create those rules.

You use menus and windows...

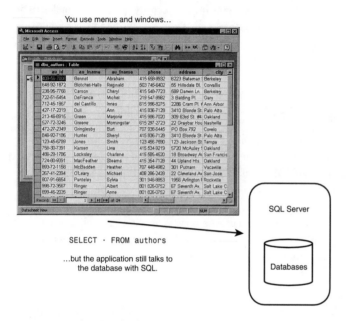

SELECT · FROM authors

...but the application still talks to the database with SQL.

SQL Server

Databases

FIGURE 1.2   The SQL behind the GUI.

You will see these terms in any further reading you do on databases.

SQL Server provides some additional commands and facilities as language extensions and stored procedures, of which some are not part of standard SQL and might not fit into the preceding categories neatly. This won't cause you a problem, though, so don't be concerned. You usually will only need to know what DML, DDL, and DCL are, not what kind of command you are using.

Summary

In this lesson you explored the components of SQL Server and the kinds of objects you will work with in a relational database management system. You should have a good conceptual grasp of what a relational database does for you. In the next lesson, I'll present a more detailed discussion of tables and related objects, so you can start working with data.

LESSON 2

Understanding Databases

This lesson will introduce you to the objects you use to store da *SQL Server 7 database.*

In the first lesson, I described the overall concepts behind SQL how a relational database is constructed. In this lesson, I'll go i more detail regarding the database objects that store your data a relationships between data items. At the end I will describe *con* the objects you will use to make sure your data stays consistent.

Tables

Most of the work of designing a database is in defining what *ent* be stored and how they are related to one another. The table is th structural unit of a relational database and is the physical structur will use to store the entities you define.

> **Entity**   An *entity* is a description of a real-world that you want to store information about in your database, such as a person, a business deal, or a fi cial transaction. It is composed of *attributes*, indiv information items (regarding the entity) you want keep, and *relations*, connections to other objects t the entity uses or depends upon in some way. Afte you have described the entities you wish to record your database, you plan your table structure to sto the entity's information in one or more database tables.

stored in the database itself. Almost no table you will work with contains data that is unrelated to any other data, so by handling these relations explicitly, it is easier both to create and to maintain a reliable, consistent database.

As a very simple example, consider the `employee` and `jobs` tables in the `pubs` database. Each job in the `jobs` table is identified by a unique `job_id`. Each employee in `employee` is *related* to a job by a `job_id` that is part of the employee record. This relation has to exist; if you had an employee without a job, it wouldn't make much sense.

Queries

A query is a command that you send to SQL Server through a database client program. You write these commands using the *lingua franca* of relational databases: the Structured Query Language (SQL). Every SQL command is referred to as a *query*, even though many commands don't retrieve anything (as you might expect from something called a *query*). Since nearly all modern database servers use SQL as their query language, you'll be able to use much of the SQL and database techniques in this books with other database servers, too.

Everything you do with SQL Server becomes a query at some point, though you might not actually see the query itself. You might be clicking buttons and check boxes in a graphical user interface (GUI), but the application responds to your commands by sending a query to the database behind the scenes, as shown in Figure 1.2.

Query commands can be grouped into three major categories:

- *Data definition language (DDL)*: DDL refers to the set of SQL statements you use in queries to define objects such as tables, constraints, stored procedures, and views. DDL is used to create the persistent structure and features of your database.

- *Data manipulation language (DML)*: DML, the subset of SQL you will use most of the time, is the group of statements such as `SELECT` and `INSERT` that you use to retrieve, analyze, modify, or delete data in your database. The DML statements are conceptually very simple, but they are incredibly powerful tools for working with information.

- *Data control language (DCL)*: DCL is used to define access controls on your data. As a user interacts with the database, the database server checks the user's permissions and grants or denies access to data and functions based on rules set by the administrator or the owner of the data. DCL is used to create those rules.

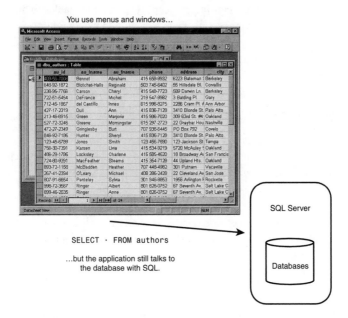

FIGURE 1.2 The SQL behind the GUI.

You will see these terms in any further reading you do on databases.

SQL Server provides some additional commands and facilities as language extensions and stored procedures, of which some are not part of standard SQL and might not fit into the preceding categories neatly. This won't cause you a problem, though, so don't be concerned. You usually will only need to know what DML, DDL, and DCL are, not what kind of command you are using.

Summary

In this lesson you explored the components of SQL Server and the kinds of objects you will work with in a relational database management system. You should have a good conceptual grasp of what a relational database does for you. In the next lesson, I'll present a more detailed discussion of tables and related objects, so you can start working with data.

LESSON 2
Understanding Databases

This lesson will introduce you to the objects you use to store data in the SQL Server 7 database.

In the first lesson, I described the overall concepts behind SQL Server and how a relational database is constructed. In this lesson, I'll go into much more detail regarding the database objects that store your data and the relationships between data items. At the end I will describe *constraints*, the objects you will use to make sure your data stays consistent.

Tables

Most of the work of designing a database is in defining what *entities* will be stored and how they are related to one another. The table is the basic structural unit of a relational database and is the physical structure you will use to store the entities you define.

 Entity   An *entity* is a description of a real-world thing that you want to store information about in your database, such as a person, a business deal, or a financial transaction. It is composed of *attributes*, individual information items (regarding the entity) you want to keep, and *relations*, connections to other objects that the entity uses or depends upon in some way. After you have described the entities you wish to record in your database, you plan your table structure to store the entity's information in one or more database tables.

A table, in SQL terms, is composed of columns and rows. Each row in
the table stores information for one entity or relation (see Figure 2.1).
Columns are the fields in each row that contain the attributes of each entity.

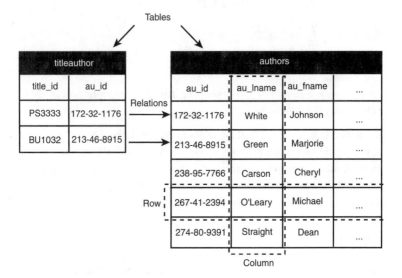

FIGURE 2.1 Database building blocks.

A table should have a set of data, ideally only a single column, that uniquely
identifies each individual row in the table. For example, because the government assures that each person's Social Security Account Number (SSAN) is
unique, the authors table in pubs uses it as the au_id to uniquely identify
the authors.

In database terms, the row identifier is called the *primary key* and is required
for most relations. Because the primary key value is used to identify the row
and will be reproduced in any index or table that references it, you should
choose the smallest reasonable data type that will accurately identify rows
in the table.

Columns

Columns store the individual pieces of data in a row of a table. Columns
have two main characteristics: their size and type. You will usually not be
concerned with the size of the column, with one exception: You cannot

create a table whose columns' sizes add up to more than 8060 bytes. This is usually not a problem; if your table has enough columns to encounter this limit, you probably should simplify it.

Tip When you design a table, keep the column count down. You rarely need a large number of columns in a normalized database table, and more than ten or fifteen often indicates that more analysis is needed.

The type of the column describes what sort of data you can store in it. Common data types you will use in SQL Server are listed in Table 2.1.

TABLE 2.1 SQL Server Data Types

Type	Description
binary(n)	Miscellaneous binary information, n bytes long
bit	A single true or false value
char(n)	Up to n letters, numbers, or punctuation characters
(small)datetime	A date, time, or both
decimal(p [,s])	An arbitrary precision floating point number allowing p significant digits with up to s to the right of the decimal
image	Large binary data
(small or tiny)int	Whole numbers
(small)money	Monetary amounts
numeric(p [,s])	General number type (same as decimal)
real(n)	General floating point type with n bits of precision

continues

TABLE 2.1 Continued

Type	Description
text	Large text objects
timestamp	Field automatically filled in with a time-based, unique counter value when a row is inserted or updated
varbinary(*n*)	Variable length binary field, up to *n* bytes
varchar(*n*)	Variable length text field, up to *n* characters

For text, char, and varchar types there are corresponding Unicode types called ntext, nchar, and nvarchar.

Unicode Unicode is an international standard for storing text that allows for many different languages. Older standards, including the modified ASCII character set used on PC-type computers, have enough characters for English and some European languages, but not languages like Chinese and Japanese. Unicode has characters for these and many other languages.

When you create a table, you tell SQL Server what kind of data each column will hold by specifying its type. This is the first of the mechanisms by which SQL Server keeps the data consistent with the database's design. This is generally a good thing, but there is a compromise between usability and efficiency. You need to select the type for a column carefully: The type should be large enough to store any reasonable value you need to store in the column, but not too large. Any extra space is wasted if it's never used. Table 2.2 lists the size and range of values for the types described in Table 2.1.

TABLE 2.2   Type Sizes and Ranges

Type	Size and Range
binary(*n*)	Fixed length of *n* bytes
bit	At least one byte; up to eight bit columns can be combined into a byte by SQL Server
char(*n*)	Fixed length of *n* bytes
(small)datetime	smalldatetime: 4 bytes, from January 1, 1900 to June 6, 2079, accurate to one minute datetime: 8 bytes, January 1, 1753 to Dec-ember 31, 9999, accurate to +/- .002 seconds
decimal(*p* [,*s*])	*p* significant digits with up to *s* digits to the right of the decimal point; requires 5 bytes if *p* < 10, 7 for *p* of 10 to 19, and 13 for *p* of 20 to 28
image, text	16 bytes; stores up to 2GB of data outside the table
(small or tiny)int	tinyint: one byte, 0-255 smallint: two bytes, -32768 to 32767 int: four bytes, +/- about 2 billion
(small)money	smallmoney: four bytes, +/- 200,000 money: eight bytes, +/- about 900 trillion
numeric(*p* [,*s*])	Generally equivalent to decimal
real(*n*)	where *n* is bits of precision; for n up to 24 (7 significant digits), 4 bytes; 8 bytes for *n* > 24 (15 significant digits)
timestamp	8 bytes
varbinary(*n*)	variable size up to 8,000 bytes, plus four bytes of overhead; *n* is maximum bytes allowed
varchar(*n*)	variable size up to 8,000 characters; *n* is maximum number of characters allowed

There is a further tradeoff in performance when using the varbinary and varchar data types. They are much more space efficient than fixed-length columns when the data will vary widely in size, but SQL Server is slowed by the need to ascertain the actual size of the data when it is retrieved. This will probably never make an impact on you, though, because for most databases storage speed is more of a limiting factor than CPU speed is.

No matter what the type of the column, it can be set to NULL if the table definition allows. NULL is a special non-value that indicates the value wasn't specified or doesn't exist. NULL is not a value, and it cannot be used in a comparison; it simply indicates nonexistence. Nullability and table definitions are explored in detail in Lesson 13, "More SQL: Defining Data."

Indices

You use an indices to speed access to data in your tables. Storing data is only part of the function of a database; retrieving it is usually an important aspect of your application, and indices make the process much faster if they are applied intelligently.

There are two kinds of indices in SQL Server: clustered and nonclustered. A *clustered* index orders the rows in the table; in other words, when you retrieve data without specifying an order in the query, the rows you see will be ordered according to the column(s) in the clustered index on the table, if one exists. Because a clustered index sets the physical order of rows, you can have only one per table. If a primary key exists, a clustered index is created on that column.

A *nonclustered* index is stored outside the table, and associates values of columns to the rows in the table, in the same way that a word index in the back of a book associates words to the pages they are used on. You would look in the index of a book on SQL to find where *query* might be defined. In the same manner, when you query SQL Server for the row in the authors table with a particular author's name (see Figure 2.2), SQL Server will use an index to find out what row in the table matches the author name, instead of looking through the table. As the figure demonstrates, an index can be built on more than one field of a table, creating a *composite index*.

Caution Text, ntext, image, bit, and computed columns cannot be indexed in SQL Server. To really work well, an index should be on a column or columns that fall somewhere between being completely unique (each row is different) and having only a small number of values (many rows share the same value). Text, ntext, image, and bit columns generally won't fit this requirement. Computed columns, which you'll see more of in Lesson 13, are based on other columns, so they don't actually store values that *could* be indexed.

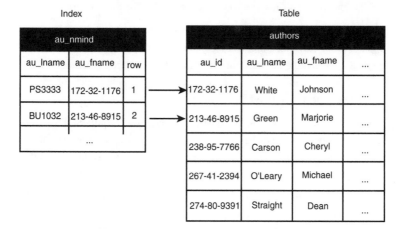

FIGURE 2.2   An indexed table.

When querying authors, which has only 23 rows, the index doesn't produce earthshaking speed improvements. With 25 million rows, on the other hand, the results can be dramatic. Because indices take up space, though, don't create them willy-nilly on your tables. There's also a performance issue; every time you update an indexed column, SQL Server has to update both the value *and* the index. Therefore, consider how people are likely to look up the data (or how your application will use the database) and create indices that support the most common queries. In Lesson 11, I'll show you how to inspect database activity to see how well your index strategy is working.

Constraints

A constraint is the second line of defense against data corruption. (Recall I said in section "Columns" earlier in this lesson that strong typing on column data was the first.) When you define a constraint, you are stating to SQL Server a rule that any data placed into a table must follow. Although constraints are usually created as part of creating the table, you can add a constraint later if existing data in the table don't violate it.

I've already described one type of constraint, a table's PRIMARY KEY. Because the primary key is defined to uniquely identify a particular row in the table, there is a corresponding constraint: You can't insert a row with the same value for the primary key as another row that already exists, and you can't insert a row without a value for the primary key.

The primary key constraint incorporates two other constraints you can put on a column: NOT NULL and UNIQUE. A NOT NULL constraint indicates to SQL Server that the column must be filled in for any row you add to the table. UNIQUE, as the name suggests, states that the value in the column cannot be repeated in two rows in the table.

The just-as-aptly named CHECK constraint provides a formula SQL Server uses to verify data values before they are inserted or updated in the table. For example, a CHECK condition like qty >= 0 on the sales table would instruct SQL Server to disallow inserting a negative sales quantity.

A DEFAULT specifies a value that will be recorded in a column if you don't supply a value or set it to NULL. Finally, a FOREIGN KEY constraint identifies columns that reference a primary key in another table. Foreign keys are described next, as I discuss relations. (See Lesson 13, "More SQL: Defining Data," for a detailed discussion on using constraints.)

Relations

I've emphasized the importance of relations to the database, but I haven't talked about how they are implemented. It won't take long to describe, though, and then I'll be done with this lesson.

Relations record dependencies and associations between tables in the database. This is part of keeping your data consistent, as it makes the associations explicit; you use SQL Server to enforce the rules instead of relying on (potentially buggy) application code. My experience has been that this mechanism, called *declarative referential integrity* (DRI), is the only reliable way to keep references consistent. There are three kinds of relations possible between tables (see Figure 2.3):

- *One-to-one*: A one-to-one relation indicates that one row in a table will be associated to one row in another; this is a rare model.

- *One-to-many*: A one-to-many relation, the most common, indicates that the referencing table (the *child* table) can have many rows that refer to a single row in the other table (the *parent* table).

- *Many-to-many*: A many-to-many relation, which should have an intermediate table to store the relationship, associates one or more records in one table to one or more in the other.

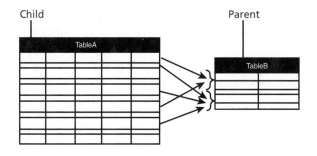

A one-to-many relation

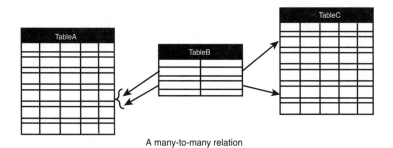

A many-to-many relation

FIGURE 2.3   Relations among tables.

Parent and Child Tables   In a relation, one table refers to another table. The table that contains the reference is called the child table, and the table it refers to is called the parent table.

Declaring a relation is simple. The parent table in the relation must have a primary key or unique column defined. In the child table, you must define a column of type identical to the primary key or unique column in the parent table. To establish the relation, you add a FOREIGN KEY constraint to the child table's column that names the parent table and key column. After the relation is established, SQL Server will check inserts and updates to the child table and reject any that violate the constraint.

Summary

That was exciting, wasn't it? Okay, maybe not, but I hope it was informative. I covered a lot of ground in this lesson, including tables, columns, data types, indices, constraints, and relations. You've seen all the major items you will store in a SQL Server database now. Make sure you're comfortable with what I've discussed before you move on.

LESSON 3

Finding Information in the Database

This lesson will introduce you to the Structured Query Language (SQL) and show you how to find data in tables using the SELECT SQL command.

Now that you've seen what is in the database, you can move on to some hands-on work. This lesson walks you through retrieving data from the database. Because I use the pubs database for the examples, you can execute the queries on your own computer and see the results as you read. After you're familiar with retrievals, you'll be ready to move on to adding and modifying data.

Understanding Structured Query Language (SQL)

SQL is a deceptively simple language used to interact with relational databases. Both SQL and the RDBMS have their roots in research at IBM from the middle 1960s through the early 1970s. With widely differing query languages on the market, the American National Standards Institute (ANSI) published a SQL standard in 1989, and then revised it in 1992. The 1992 standard, ANSI X3.135-1992, is the current version, and is usually referred to as SQL2 or, most commonly, SQL92.

I call SQL "deceptively simple." Why? SQL has only a few keywords compared to any other programming language you will encounter, but this apparently minimalist set of commands can, with some forethought on your part, perform complicated analysis and transformation of data. If this is your first encounter with SQL, you'll be amazed at what you can do when you're done with this book.

The SELECT Statement

Absolutely *the* most common statement you'll use in SQL, the SELECT statement retrieves data from tables, views, and built-in functions in SQL Server. The syntax for SELECT is as follows:

```
SELECT { * ¦ columnref [, columnref ... ] }
FROM tableref [, tableref ...]
[[INNER ¦ {LEFT ¦ RIGHT} OUTER ]
JOIN tableref ON columnref = columnref ...]
[WHERE expression [{AND ¦ OR} expression ...]]
```

The component *columnref* is the name of a column, *tableref* is the name of a table, and *expression* is a criterion that is either true or false. Got that?

Okay, maybe I should explain a little. The syntax description format I'll use in this book is similar to that used by Microsoft, so you'll see almost the same thing here as you will when you use Books Online:

- Items that are required are outside any brackets or braces.

- Items that are optional are enclosed in brackets.

- Items that are literal (you should type them verbatim) are in a normal font.

- Items that should be replaced with your own data are in italics.

- If you can use one of a list of items, the choices are separated by a vertical bar, called a *pipe* (¦).

- Mandatory choice within a choice (you must include one or the other) is enclosed in braces ({}).

The main change I make to the Books Online format is to use the ellipsis points to signify that the items in a set of brackets can be repeated.

The description of the SELECT syntax says you must have at least the word SELECT; either an asterisk (*) or one or more *columnref*s (the *SELECT list*); the word FROM, and at least one *tableref*.

After the FROM, you *can* include JOINs, each of which must contain the keyword JOIN, a *tableref*, the keyword ON, and a statement of the equivalent columns (the *columnref*s). Within the JOIN clause, you can additionally specify INNER, LEFT OUTER, or RIGHT OUTER to modify the type of join. The ellipsis points at the end of the JOIN clause indicate it can be repeated as often as you like.

Finally, you can include a WHERE keyword, followed by conditional expressions separated by the AND or OR keywords, to limit the rows returned.

This representation of SELECT only shows part of the statement; you'll get the whole thing in Lesson 12, "Analyzing Your Data with SQL," when you've seen a little more of the database. In the remainder of the lesson, you're going to see how to use each of the elements shown previously.

Before you go through the examples, you'll have to bring up the SQL Server Query Analyzer. You should find it in the Microsoft SQL Server 7.0 menu on your Start menu. When it starts, log in to the database as your network requires. To use the pubs database, select it in the DB drop-down list under the menu bar at the top of the window (see Figure 3.1).

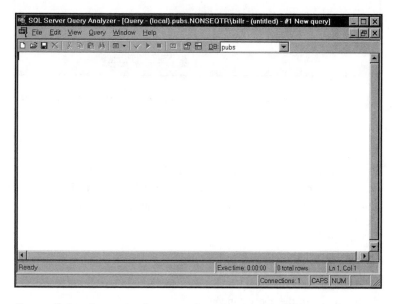

FIGURE 3.1   Query Analyzer ready to work with pubs.

I'm going to use the authors, titles, and titleauthor tables for the examples in this lesson. Figure 3.2 shows the tables and relationship

between them. You can also execute `sp_help tablename` in Query
Analyzer to show information on a table.

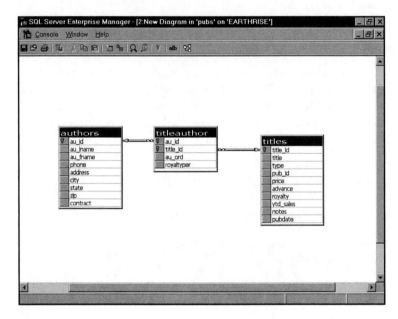

FIGURE 3.2   Titles, Authors, and Titleauthor Tables in SQL Server 7.

Using SELECT

The simplest SELECT you can execute, as indicated by the syntax description, retrieves everything from one table. Execute the following in Query
Analyzer by typing it into the text area of your query window and clicking
the Play button:

```
SELECT *
FROM   authors
```

When you execute the query, you'll see data resembling the following in
the lower half of the query window:

au_id	au_lname	au_fname	...
172-32-1176	White	Johnson	...
213-46-8915	Green	Marjorie	...
238-95-7766	Carson	Cheryl	...
.			
.			
899-46-2035	Ringer	Anne	...
998-72-3567	Ringer	Albert	...

I've abbreviated the output to save space; if you tried out the query, you know why. It produces a lot of data, which might or might not be useful to you. That's why you usually won't use an unconstrained "give me everything" query like this.

To restrict the data you get, just look up the authors' names. Use the following query:

```
SELECT  au_fname, au_lname
FROM    authors
```

This produces the somewhat more manageable output that follows:

au_fname	au_lname
Abraham	Bennet
Reginald	Blotchet-Halls
Cheryl	Carson
.	
.	
Johnson	White
Akiko	Yokomoto

Instead of the asterisk, this SELECT specifies the columns you want to see in the SELECT list. It still retrieves every row in the table, though.

 Tip SQL gives you a lot of latitude in how specific you have to be. It's very easy to type SELECT * FROM tablename, but the more specific you are in any SQL statement, the better the database is going to serve you and the other users on the system.

Using WHERE and Logical Expressions

To get more specific in retrieving data, introduce the WHERE clause. WHERE is used to specify criteria that rows must meet to be returned. The keyword is followed by one or more expressions, each of which contains a column; an operator; and another column, expression, or value.

> **Operator**   In SQL Server, it is a symbol or keyword that relates or changes one or more *operands*. You are probably familiar with *arithmetic* operators for addition (+), subtraction (-), and so on. SQL Server provides these operators and many others.

The operators you use in WHERE expressions are the relational and logical operators. Expressions using these operators can be either true or false, depending on the operands. Some common expressions of this type are shown in Table 3.1 (see Books Online for the full set). In general, the operands in these comparisons must be of the same type for the comparison to be valid.

TABLE 3.1   Common Comparisons

This expression...	is true if...
x = y	x and y are the same value
x <> y	x and y are not the same value
x > y	x is greater than y
x IS NULL	x is not defined (x is null)
x BETWEEN y AND z	x is in the range [y..z]
x IN (a, b, ...)	x is in the set of values
x LIKE y	the data in x resembles the pattern in y

For example, to look up Charlene Locksley's telephone number, you execute the following query:

```
SELECT au_fname, au_lname, phone
FROM    authors
WHERE   au_fname = 'Charlene'
  AND   au_lname = 'Locksley'
```

This query produces the following:

```
au_fname                    au_lname               phone
--------------------        --------------------   -----------
Charlene                    Locksley               415 585-4620
```

LIKE and Wildcards

The last operator I'll demonstrate explicitly, LIKE, is used to match patterns in character data like the author names in authors. In the previous example, you tested for an exact match to Ms. Locksley's name. If you didn't know how her name was spelled, just that it started with *L*, you could use the following query:

```
SELECT au_fname, au_lname, phone
FROM    authors
WHERE au_lname LIKE 'L%'
```

This query produces the exact same output as the previous one, but if there were more than one person whose last name started with the letter *L,* they would all have been listed.

The LIKE keyword in the expression is followed by a pattern that SQL Server compares to candidate rows to include or exclude them. The pattern in the example, 'L%', tells SQL Server to show any rows whose au_lname starts with the capital *L*. The percent sign in the pattern indicates any number of any other characters can appear after the *L*. If you're familiar with DOS wildcards, the percent sign is equivalent to the DOS asterisk.

You can use two other wildcard items in the pattern. An underscore allows any one character: 'L_' would match *Lu* and *Li* but not *Locksley*. The last item is a range specification; if you wanted to retrieve names starting with *A* through *D*, you could specify "au_lname LIKE '[A-D]%'", in which the expression in brackets indicates the range of values that will match in this position.

There are far too many operators available to demonstrate here; those listed in Table 3.1 will be the ones you probably use most often, and you should have the hang of using them now. Try experimenting with queries on the authors table if you'd like to see more of how they work.

Inner Joins

You're finally going to see one way relations are used in a database. When you retrieve data from more than one table using a relation to associate the data, you instruct the database to *join* the tables based on the criteria you specify. Some databases will join tables automatically if the references are defined, but this is not standard behavior. In standard SQL, you start your select from a *base* table, and then link additional tables using the JOIN clause of the SELECT statement to tell SQL Server how to correlate rows from the tables.

For example, imagine you want to retrieve a list of authors whose names start with *B* and the books they have written. The base table you'll use is the authors table. I'll start the query with just the authors and titleauthor tables so you get a feel for *incremental refinement* as well as learn how the join works.

 Incremental Refinement   The technique of starting a simple query and then adding to it is called *incremental refinement*. It is a much better approach than trying to get an involved query to work in one step. Incremental refinement makes it much easier to get the syntax and results you need by attacking the problem a little at a time.

Type the following:

```
SELECT au_fname, au_lname, title_id
FROM authors
INNER JOIN titleauthor ON authors.au_id = titleauthor.au_id
WHERE au_lname LIKE 'B%'
```

This query produces the following output:

au_fname	au_lname	title_id
Abraham	Bennet	BU1032
Reginald	Blotchet-Halls	TC4203

If you look at the data in the two tables, you can verify that the title IDs shown are the ones in `titleauthor` that are associated to authors, that is, in which the au_id foreign key in `titleauthor` matches the author's au_id primary key in `authors`. The inner join both includes the `titleauthor` table in the result set (notice that the column `title_id` in the SELECT list comes from the `titleauthor` table) and tells SQL Server that it should match rows from `titleauthor` and `authors` by comparing the au_id values.

Because columns in both authors and `titleauthor` are called au_id, they are identified as authors.au_id and `titleauthor`.au_id. This dotted notation resolves name ambiguities for SQL Server by specifying which au_id you're talking about. I'll get into this more in Lesson 12, "Analyzing Your Data with SQL." For now, just remember to use this *tablename.columnname* syntax when there are multiple columns with the same name in your queries.

The query is supposed to show the book titles, though, so it needs to join another table, `titles`. The following query does the trick:

```
SELECT au_fname, au_lname, title
FROM authors
INNER JOIN titleauthor ON authors.au_id = titleauthor.au_id
INNER JOIN titles ON titleauthor.title_id = titles.title_id
WHERE au_lname LIKE 'B%'
```

From this query, you finally get the output required:

au_fname	au_lname	title
Abraham	Bennet	The Busy Executive's Database...
Reginald	Blotchet-Halls	Fifty Years in Buckingham Palace...

I changed the `title_id` column in the SELECT list to `title` (the name of the field from the `titles` table that I wanted). Then, I added a join from `titleauthor` to the `titles` table; the original join matched authors to the title id, but the new join connects through the title id to the title in `titles`.

Outer Joins

The examples so far have used the INNER JOIN to retrieve only those rows that had matching keys. An outer join, on the other hand, can include rows from one table that don't have matching rows in the other. To show this, I'll change the query to retrieve *all* authors whose names start with *G*, and any books that they have published. Using outer joins, you'll see authors that haven't published, as well as those who have. The following example demonstrates the query and its results:

```
SELECT au_fname, au_lname, title
FROM authors
LEFT OUTER JOIN titleauthor
ON authors.au_id = titleauthor.au_id
LEFT OUTER JOIN titles
ON titleauthor.title_id = titles.title_id
WHERE au_lname LIKE 'G%'
```

au_fname	au_lname	title
Marjorie	Green	The Busy Executive's Database Guide
Marjorie	Green	You Can Combat Computer Stress!
Morningstar	Greene	(null)
Burt	Gringlesby	Sushi, Anyone?

The LEFT OUTER JOIN in place of the INNER JOIN tells SQL Server to include all columns in the *left* table, even if there isn't a match in the *right* table. In the first join, this says to keep rows in the authors table that don't match rows in titleauthor; the second has to be an outer join as well, or SQL Server will eliminate the authors without titles for not matching any rows in the titles table. With this query, you see Morningstar Greene's name, though this author hasn't published anything. (See the (null) in the title column?)

Transact SQL Versus ANSI SQL92

Transact SQL, the form of SQL used in SQL Server, is not the same as ANSI SQL. Each version of SQL Server provides better ANSI conformance than the last, but a problem arises as it evolves. References and tutorials for SQL Server can use older dialects of SQL, so the ANSI SQL query you used in a previous example

```
SELECT au_fname, au_lname, title_id
FROM authors
INNER JOIN titleauthor ON authors.au_id = titleauthor.au_id
WHERE au_lname LIKE 'L%'
```

might be demonstrated in another reference as

```
SELECT au_fname, au_lname, title_id
FROM   authors, titleauthor
WHERE authors.au_id = titleauthor.au_id
  AND au_lname LIKE 'L%'
```

This syntax mixes the joining expression with the criteria used to identify which rows you want to retrieve and is anachronistic. SQL Server allows both forms, but you should use the ANSI JOIN syntax, if only because it is clearer, by identifying joins separate from selection criteria.

Other differences exist between Transact SQL and ANSI; I'll note them as I encounter them. If you use other SQL references, keep an eye out for these inconsistencies, and you'll be okay.

Summary

You covered a lot in this lesson. You have learned about syntax: SELECTing data from the database, wildcard matches and logical expressions, joins, and incremental refinement as a tool to build queries. Are you ready for a break?

This is probably the hardest lesson. I've introduced a lot of new concepts in a very short period, but if you've followed along you're in good shape for the rest of the book. Many of the concepts I discussed here are going to be reused and reinforced in following lessons because the information you've been working with in this lesson applies to many other areas of SQL Server.

Remember: To query multiple tables, you started with one table and then added tables by joining them across relations. The columns you retrieved in the SELECT list came from any of the tables in the FROM and JOIN elements, but when you encountered multiple columns with the same name, you had to use the dotted *table.column* syntax.

In the next lesson, you're going to complete your knowledge of basic SQL by adding, updating, and deleting data in the database. With your knowledge from this chapter it will be a breeze. After that, you'll be able to move into the application-oriented lessons, where you'll see how to put your database knowledge to work by using data from the pub databawse in applications like Microsoft Word and Excel and by publishing it to the Web.

LESSON 4

Adding and Changing Data

In this lesson, you'll learn how to add data to your database and change or delete existing data.

Now you're going to start adding and changing data using the DML statements INSERT, UPDATE, and DELETE. With your knowledge of SELECT, you'll find these new commands easy to understand. I'll round the lesson out with *transactions*, an important component in keeping your database in good repair.

Data Manipulation Language (DML)

DML includes commands for creating, updating, retrieving, and deleting data. These abilities may seem modest, but they are anything but. As you will see, they can do wonders with your data.

INSERT

INSERT is used to create new rows in a table. The syntax you'll need is as follows:

```
INSERT [ INTO ] tableref [ ( columnref [, columnref ... ] ) ]
{ VALUES({DEFAULT ¦ NULL ¦ expression }
    [,{DEFAULT ¦ NULL ¦ expression } ...])
  ¦ SELECT ... }
```

You have to have INSERT followed by *tableref*, VALUES, and the values to insert in parentheses, separated by commas. As indicated in the syntax, you can also use data from a SELECT, but don't worry about that yet.

Some databases require you to include the INTO keyword, but SQL Server does not. You can include an explicit list of the columns after the *tableref*, and I strongly urge you to do so. In some cases it's mandatory, and it's always a good way to make it clear what columns the VALUES are going into.

Try the following in Query Analyzer:

```
SELECT count(*) FROM authors
```

It will produce this output:

```
-----------
23
```

The count(*) is a function you can use in the SELECT list to retrieve the number of matching rows instead of the rows themselves. The output from the query indicates there are 23 rows in the authors table. To add another row, execute the following:

```
INSERT authors
VALUES( '123-45-6789', 'Jones', 'Smith', '123 456-7890',
    '123 Main St.', 'Someplace', 'NY', '12345', 1 )
```

If you count the rows again, you'll find there are 24 rows in authors now.

> **Note** I'll show you DELETE later, but if you try these statements, run the following to remove each row you insert before you try another:
>
> ```
> DELETE authors
> WHERE  au_id = '123-45-6789'
> ```

This INSERT demonstrates clearly why I counsel you to include the column list after the table name in your INSERT, even when SQL Server doesn't require it. The command you entered supplies values for each of the columns in authors, in order. So, without looking up the data in the database, tell me: which is the new author's first name, 'Smith' or 'Jones?'

Far better for you and anyone else who has to look at your SQL is the following:

```
INSERT authors ( au_id, au_lname, au_fname, phone, address,
        city, state, zip, contract )
VALUES( '123-45-6789', 'Jones', 'Smith', '123 456-7890',
        '123 Main St.', 'Someplace', 'NY', '12345', 1 )
```

The column list after the table name lists all the columns you will supply data for in the VALUES list, in the same order. This way no one gets confused;

it's obvious that I'm talking to Mr. Jones, not Mr. Smith. Also, by naming
the columns explicitly, you can provide them in any order: You don't have to
list them in the order they are defined in the table. (What if it really *was* Mr.
Smith?) And you only need to include the columns you want to.

NULLs and DEFAULTs

You can use two keywords in place of a value in the VALUES list, either
NULL or DEFAULT. If you don't have the data for a column, and the column
is not required (in other words, if it doesn't have a NOT NULL constraint on
it), you can use NULL instead of a value to show that the information is
unknown.

Without NULL, you would have to resort to a *magic value*, a value you
think will never be valid in your data, like -1 or 9999. These can mark
a column if data isn't available, but they sometimes come back to haunt
you. In some older applications, for example, programmers used all nines
in date fields as a magic number. Unfortunately for the software's current
users, the date 9/9/99 isn't so far off anymore. NULL makes this kind of
error unlikely.

The system stored procedure sp_help *objectname* displays a description
of any object in a database. Use the following SQL to display the authors
table's columns, constraints, storage locations, and other information:

```
sp_help authors
```

In the column descriptions, under the heading Nullable (you may have
to scroll right a bit), you'll see yes for the address, city, state, and zip
columns, indicating these columns accept nulls. If you don't have the
address for an author, you can use NULL in place of the values for these
columns:

```
INSERT authors ( au_id, au_lname, au_fname, phone, address,
        city, state, zip, contract )
VALUES( '123-45-6789', 'Jones', 'Smith', '123 456-7890', NULL,
        NULL, NULL, NULL, 1 )
```

To retrieve data from the table where the ZIP wasn't specified, you can use
the IS NULL criterion in your SELECT statement. (You *cannot*, however, use
WHERE zip = NULL.)

```
SELECT au_id, au_fname, au_lname
FROM    authors
WHERE   zip IS NULL
```

After inserting the no-address author, this query produces the following results:

```
au_id        au_fname              au_lname
-----------  --------------------  --------------------------
123-45-6789 Smith                  Jones
```

Try using a default now: Delete that row, and then modify the previous insert to change the telephone number value to DEFAULT:

```
INSERT authors ( au_id, au_lname, au_fname, phone, address,
         city, state, zip, contract )
VALUES( '123-45-6789', 'Jones', 'Smith', DEFAULT, NULL,
         NULL, NULL, NULL, 1 )
```

Now use SELECT to retrieve the row you inserted:

```
SELECT au_fname, au_lname, phone
FROM    authors
WHERE   zip IS NULL
```

This results in the following output:

```
au_fname        au_lname                        phone
-------------  ------------------------------  ------------
Smith           Jones                           UNKNOWN
```

If you use sp_help to describe authors, you see a DEFAULT constraint on the phone column. If you either include the DEFAULT keyword for the value, or leave the column out of the INSERT altogether, SQL Server will use the value specified in the DEFAULT constraint. In this case, the default for the phone column is "UNKNOWN," as you see in the results.

Copying Data with INSERT

The last form of INSERT is probably the most interesting, and gives a glimpse of how powerful SQL can be. When you insert into a table, you can specify one row as I did previously, but it doesn't have to be that way. At its heart, SQL just wants to work with tables, and the previous INSERT statements have been working with a special case: The VALUES list is essentially a table with only one row.

When you execute a SELECT statement, you create a special, transient table called a *result set*. For the SELECT statements you've been running, the result set is displayed on your screen, but that's not all you can do. You can also use that result set as the data values to insert into another table by using the SELECT statement in place of the VALUES list. For example, if you have another table that stores "people" with their names and addresses, you can use the following query to copy your authors from authors to people:

```
INSERT people( fname, lname, address, city, state, zip )
    SELECT au_fname, au_lname, address, city, state, zip
    FROM authors
```

Note This example uses a table called "people" that doesn't exist in the pubs table. If you have permission to create tables, you can create it with the following DDL:

```
CREATE TABLE people (
    lname varchar     (40)     NOT NULL ,
    fname varchar     (20)     NOT NULL ,
    address varchar   (40)     NULL ,
    city varchar      (20)     NULL ,
    state char        (2)      NULL ,
    zip char          (5)      NULL ,
)
```

When you're finished with the lesson, clean up by deleting it with this command:

```
DROP TABLE people
```

I'll discuss these commands in Lesson 13, "More SQL: Defining Data."

In this INSERT, the inner SELECT statement creates a result set with six columns (as specified in the SELECT list) and as many rows as are in the authors table. The rows in the result set are then fed into the INSERT as the values that go into the people table. The result is the same as if you typed 24 INSERT statements, each with a VALUES list containing the data from one row in the authors table.

The inner SELECT can contain any valid SQL for retrieving data, as long as it produces a result set with the right number and type of columns, as named in the outer INSERT statement. The values you insert can be drawn or calculated from any table or other data source you can retrieve through a SELECT. With this and the similar capability in UPDATE, you can use SQL to transform your data in any manner you require.

UPDATE

UPDATE modifies existing rows in a table. You have to tell SQL Server what table and columns to update and what the new values are. The following is the syntax you'll use:

```
UPDATE tableref
SET    columnref = { expression ¦ DEFAULT ¦ NULL }
    [, columnref =  { expression ¦ DEFAULT ¦ NULL } ... ]
[ FROM tableref [, tableref ... ]
[ WHERE expression  [ { AND ¦ OR } expression ... ]]
```

With the example row from the INSERT discussion, you can execute the following to give the author a telephone number:

```
UPDATE authors
SET phone = '123 456-7890'
WHERE au_id = '123-45-6789'
```

UPDATE will scan the table and, in every row that matches the WHERE expression, it will update the columns as directed in the SET list. You can use DEFAULT and NULL, as well, in a manner similar to INSERT:

```
UPDATE authors
SET phone = DEFAULT
WHERE au_id = '123-45-6789'
```

You just can't make it any simpler than that. So let's complicate things by updating from other tables.

If you've been running the example queries as you went along, you have an author, Mr. Jones, who is recorded in the authors and people tables, but with no address information in either place. If you set his address with the following SQL, you update the authors table, but people is still not set:

```
UPDATE authors
SET    address = '123 Jackson St.',
       city = 'Tampa',
```

```
        state = 'FL',
        zip = '23450'
WHERE   au_fname='Smith'
  AND   au_lname = 'Jones'
```

This sets the address for the row that meets both of the criteria in the WHERE clause of the command; using the AND operator tells SQL Server that a row must meet *both* criteria before it will be updated.

Now that you've updated authors, you'll want to fix people, too. So how do you propagate the updates to the people table from authors?

It's so simple, it's scary:

```
UPDATE  people
SET     people.address = authors.address,
        people.city = authors.city,
        people.state = authors.state,
        people.zip = authors.zip
FROM    authors
WHERE   people.fname = authors.au_fname
  AND   people.lname = authors.au_lname
```

This is the same concept as inserting data from a table into another, but it's a little longer because it has to tell SQL Server how to match rows from the source table to the destination. In the example, the UPDATE line identifies the table that will be updated. The SET section tells SQL Server how to update the target table; in this case, it is a simple copy from each field in authors to the corresponding field in people. The FROM line tells SQL Server that the source data will come from authors.

Finally, the criteria in the WHERE tell SQL Server how to match rows in the two tables; here, you tell it to copy data between rows whose first and last names match. Ideally, you'd match primary keys across the tables, but when you use this kind of update, there's no guarantee you'll have the primary key in both tables (as in this example).

As with INSERT, the values that are assigned to the columns in the target table (people) do not have to be the direct match you see here. You can use functions, arithmetic operators, or any other valid expression for the values used to update the target.

DELETE

After INSERT and UPDATE, DELETE seems pedestrian. The syntax is simple:

```
DELETE [FROM] tableref
[WHERE expression [ { AND ¦ OR } expression ... ] ]
```

Nope, there's nothing hidden here. That's all there is to DELETE. SQL Server will delete any rows in the table named by *tableref* that match the *expression* list in the WHERE. The only thing you really have to worry about is accidentally executing the following:

```
DELETE FROM my_really_important_table
```

As you might guess, this deletes *all* the data in the table.

Transactions

The basic unit of work in the database is a *transaction*. Each time you change anything in the database, a transaction is written to a log so that SQL Server can replicate, undo or redo the changes to keep the database clean, or supply the changes to other servers. A transaction that is in progress can be either *committed* or *rolled back* to apply or discard changes, respectively.

You can use your own transactions to manage your work as well. Right now, I'm going to show you how to use a transaction to try out a DELETE without actually performing it. Listing 4.1 demonstrates an aborted transaction.

LISTING 4.1   Using a Transaction to Test a DELETE

```
BEGIN TRANSACTION

DELETE titleauthor

SELECT count(*)
FROM titleauthor

ROLLBACK

SELECT count(*)
FROM titleauthor
```

This produces the following output:

```
(25 row(s) affected)


- - - - - - - - - - -
0

(1 row(s) affected)


- - - - - - - - - - -
25

(1 row(s) affected)
```

The SQL starts a transaction with BEGIN TRANSACTION. The very next statement in the batch deletes all the associations from titleauthor (note the "25 rows affected" in the output). Next, I count the rows in the table to show you that yes, all the records are gone, producing the zero result next in the output. All is not lost, though. The ROLLBACK that comes next in the SQL undoes the DELETE statement, as you can see in the result from the last SELECT count(*), which shows that all 25 rows are back in place. Without the ROLLBACK, or with a COMMIT TRANSACTION in its place, the data would be completely lost.

In your time with SQL Server, you will use transactions for a lot more than this little demonstration implies, but you should remember this when you are modifying data in the database. If you aren't sure what the effect of a command will be, try it out inside a transaction, display the results, and roll back at the end.

Summary

That was a lot of information, but it should be getting easier now. In this lesson, you have learned how to use DML to update your database by putting new data in, modifying existing data, and using information already in the database to populate new tables.

Congratulations! You've learned a lot, and you're ready to do some real work with SQL Server. I'm going to switch gears and show you how to put your knowledge into practice with some other applications. In the next few lessons, you'll use data in documents, spreadsheets, and even on the Web

LESSON 5
Using Data in Microsoft Word

This lesson teaches you how to use the merge features of Microsoft Word to create letters and forms from database data.

Is there any business correspondence more derided than the form letter? I don't think so. In the past, bulk mailings were so poorly executed that the intent of customizing them to each customer was lost—you could tell it was a form letter, often just by the fact that the recipient's name was lost in the middle of a large blank! Rather than making the customer feel a personal touch, these machine-generated mailings epitomized *im*personality.

Times have changed. As you will see, Microsoft Word provides merge capabilities for creating these materials that can produce high-quality, personal-appearing documents with only a small amount of effort.

Note For the lessons in this chapter and the next, you must be using Office97 Service Release 2 (SR-2), and you must have installed MS Query. MS Query is included with Office 97, but it isn't installed by default. If it isn't on your computer, either install it yourself or ask an information systems support person to do so for you. If you add the program after installing the SR-2 patch, you must apply the patch again.

Defining Your Query

Before you create the merge document, you must create a data source that connects to the database, and then a query file that says how to get data from this data source. In this section, you'll connect to the server and define a query to retrieve author name and address information to use in your document.

In this context, a data source refers to an *Open Database Connectivity (ODBC) Data Source Name (DSN)*, a record you create with Control Panel's ODBC Data Sources applet. A DSN holds the information you need to connect to a database, so you can use it in several applications without having to set it up again and again. I'll show you the basic steps for setting up a data source here, but I won't go into a lot of detail. (See Peter Debetta, et al., *Microsoft SQL Server 7 Programming Unleashed*, second edition (Indianapolis: Sams Publishing, 1999), which has extensive descriptions of this and other interfaces to SQL Server.)

You're going to use MS Query to create your query definition for Word. This little application isn't included on the Start menu items that Office Setup creates, so you'll have to go to the Office program directly (typically *somedriveletter*:\Program Files\Microsoft Office) and find the Microsoft Query shortcut. You can copy this to your desktop or personal menu tree if you like.

Defining the Data Source

You can create a *user* DSN, a *system* DSN, or a *file* DSN; in general, user DSNs are available only to you, whereas a system or file DSN is available to others using your computer. You can also copy file DSNs across the network so others can use them. In this exercise, you'll create a user DSN named pubs.

Follow these steps to create a data source:

1. Open Control Panel's ODBC Data Sources applet and click the User DSN tab (see Figure 5.1). Click the Add button to display the Create New Data Source window.

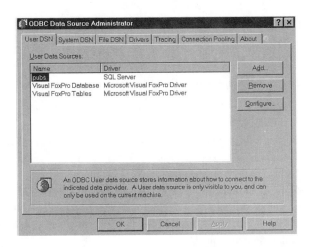

FIGURE 5.1   User DSNs in the ODBC Data Source Administrator.

2. Select the SQL Server driver and click Finish.

3. In the first page of the SQL Server DSN Configuration dialog, Figure 5.2, type in the name for the data source (use pubs for this example), a description if you like, and either type the name of the server your database is on or choose it from the drop-down list. Click Next.

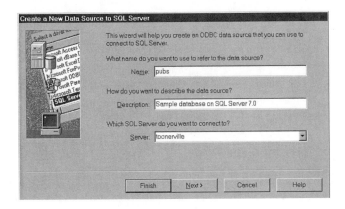

FIGURE 5.2   Describing the data source.

4. Set your login information according to your site policy; if you use SQL Server authentication, you'll need to type your Login

ID and Password in the spaces provided. Make sure the Connect to SQL Server option at the bottom is selected and click Next.

5. Click the Change the Default Database to: check box, select pubs from the drop-down list of databases, and then click Next.

6. Click Finish on the last page without changing anything.

When you finish these steps, ODBC will show you the ODBC Microsoft SQL Server Setup window (see Figure 5.3) that recaps the options you've set (or that it supplied) and lets you test the data source. After you have done so, you should receive a dialog box showing you steps followed by a successful completion message. Press OK on that window, as well as OK on the setup window. You're back in the data sources window with the new pubs data source in the list.

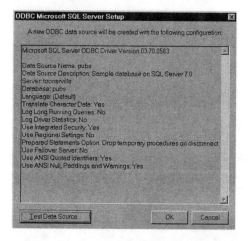

FIGURE 5.3   ODBC's recap of your connection description.

 Caution   Some applications let you store your user ID and password in the DSN so you don't have to supply them when you connect to the database. Do not do this! When you do, not only can others use your DSN to get into the database (under your ID), they can also steal your password by looking in the DSN.

Building the Query

Now you can specify the query data you're going to retrieve. Follow these steps:

1. Open MS Query and click the New Query icon (the first one on the toolbar), which shows the Choose Data Source window (see Figure 5.4).

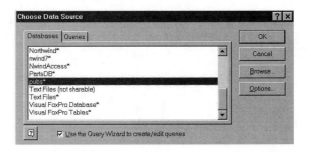

FIGURE 5.4 Choosing the data source for MS Query.

2. Select the pubs data source you just created. Click OK and log in to the database if asked. You will see the Query Wizard window (see Figure 5.5). The left side shows the tables and views in the database, and the right shows the columns you've selected to retrieve.

3. Click the plus box next to authors to expand it, then double-click au_fname, au_lname, address, city, state, and zip to retrieve those columns. When you're done, your display should resemble Figure 5.5.

4. Click Next to move on, and then click it again because you aren't going to specify retrieval filters. Because it doesn't really matter what order the data are retrieved for a merge, just click Finish to complete the step.

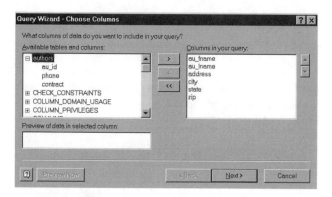

FIGURE 5.5   Query Wizard ready to retrieve Author addresses.

You're done creating the query, so save it to a .qry file in the directory where you're creating documents. MS Query will save the file with a .dqy extension by default; therefore, you have to change the type using the Save as Type drop-down menu in the Save As dialog box. Exit MS Query when you're done.

Tip   You don't have to run MS Query independently from Word to create a data source; you can create one directly into your application when you set up the merge document. However, if you create the query and save it as a file outside of Word, you can use it with other documents later.

Linking Data to Your Document

The next step is to create the document you're going to bring the data into. You do this in Word, of course, using the Mail Merge option on the Tools menu. One idiosyncrasy of this interface is that although it lets you create a new document to merge into or use an existing one, you can't access the feature if you don't already have a document open.

Open Word and click the new document icon on the toolbar to create a new blank document (if it doesn't do so by itself). Type a boilerplate letter; Figure 5.6 shows the example I used. Notice that there's no address for the recipient, and the salutation has only the greeting followed by a space and a comma: You will let Word get the recipient's name and address from SQL Server.

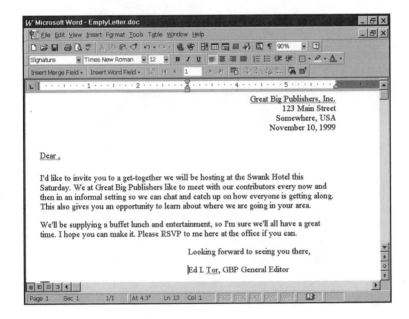

FIGURE 5.6 Example merge document in Word.

Now that you have the letter that you're going to send out framed, bring up the Mail Merge Helper with the Mail Merge option on the Tools menu. The helper window is shown in Figure 5.7. This window helps walk you through the process of creating the merge document by ordering the tasks you need to accomplish.

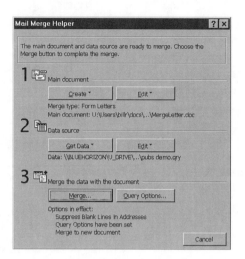

FIGURE 5.7   Word's Mail Merge Helper showing tasks in sequence.

Follow these steps to import the data to your Word template:

1. Click the Create button and choose Form Letters from the drop-down menu that appears. On the dialog box Word responds with, click the Active Window button to use the letter you created. The Helper window changes to show the type of merge and the name of the document you're using.

2. Data Source in the Helper is where you tell Word what data to use. When you click the Get Data button, the resulting drop-down has Create Data Source... and Open Data Source... options; use the Open option. On the Open Data Source window, change the Files of Type option to MS Query Files (*.qry) and select the query file you created in the last section. Click Yes to the next dialog box so you won't have to respecify the query later.

3. Word now tells you that you haven't added any merge fields to your document. Because you haven't put any in, this isn't a big surprise. Click Edit Main Document to proceed.

4. You've done all the hard work. Now all you need to do is put the cursor in your document where you want a merge field (a column from the query), and then click Insert Merge Field on the toolbar. You can select any of the columns that are in the query from the

drop-down list. Word will put a field into your document, at the
cursor, which it will fill in with the data from that column when
you merge your data with the document to create the letters.

Figure 5.8 shows my letter with the fields filled in.

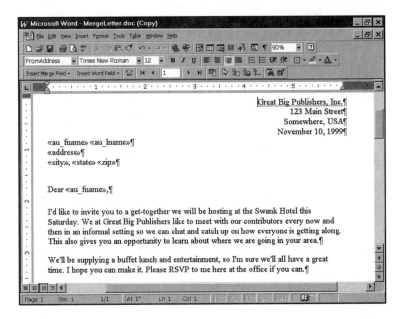

FIGURE 5.8   Merge letter with address fields and salutation.

Printing the Results

When you have the document set up to your liking, view the results by
clicking the Merge button on the Mail Merge Helper (step 3 of the dialog
in Figure 5.7). Leave Merge set to New document, and click Merge. Word
queries the database and creates a new document containing letters to all
your authors.

If the format of the document is not to your liking, close it without saving,
go back and edit the merge document, and run the merge again. Because the
results go into a new document, you can do this as many times as you like.

When you're ready to print the letters, either print the document that was created, or change the Merge To setting in the Merge dialog from New document to Printer. Now send the output directly to your printer.

Summary

I've walked you through merging data into your documents from SQL Server in this lesson. To recap, you used the following steps to create your merged documents:

1. Create or select an ODBC Data Source Name (DSN).

2. Tell Word how to query the database for data.

3. Incorporate the data into your document with Merge Fields.

The example shown, sending an announcement to a group of people, is the most common one you'll use, but there is more you can do. It is just as easy, for example, to create another merge document to print mailing labels or even envelopes for your letter by choosing a different type of merge document in the first step of the Mail Merge Helper. You can even send out emails if you have Internet addresses in the database.

In the next lesson, I'll move on to using numbers from the database in Excel. Just as Word makes it easy to communicate, you'll see that Excel's data input features give you a strong tool for analyzing data.

LESSON 6

Analyzing Numerical Data with Microsoft Excel

This lesson will teach you how to use Microsoft Excel with numeric information retrieved from your database.

Database reports, rollups, and such, periodically delivered to you or on your desktop computer, are fine as far as they go, but they're just static information. If you need to see the data from a different angle, or if you need graphics that aren't in the reports, you're stuck. Excel bridges that gap by providing for linked data in spreadsheets that draw on database queries.

The last lesson showed you how to use data in Word; using it in Excel is similar, with a few different considerations that I'll discuss. When you're finished with this lesson, you'll be able to take data from SQL Server and work with it in an Excel spreadsheet.

Defining Your Query

You've seen how to use the Query Wizard in MS Query to create a query in Lesson 5, "Using Data in Microsoft Word," but you're not restricted to just what you can point and click in the dialogs. That's a good thing; you didn't expend the effort to learn retrievals with SELECT for nothing!

This time, you're going to look at the query's SQL instead of just clicking buttons. Because you've seen how to save the queries to files, I'll skip that and create the query through Excel.

When you analyze data with Excel, you'll usually do yourself a favor if you place the raw data in one sheet and analyze it in another; that way, you don't have a lot of different types of items cluttering your sheet. For this exercise, start Excel and create a workbook with sheets named Analysis and Data.

Switch to your data sheet. To import some data from the database, follow these steps:

1. Click the Data menu, and then choose Get External Data, Create New Query.

2. In the Choose Data Source window that follows, turn off the Use the Query Wizard to create/edit queries checkbox. Choose the pubs DSN I created in the last lesson, and click OK.

3. MS Query opens with the Add Tables dialog displayed so you can pick where your data will come from. Double-click the authors, titleauthor, and sales tables. Notice that the tables are automatically connected with join lines showing the relations between them. Figure 6.1 shows MS Query with the tables added.

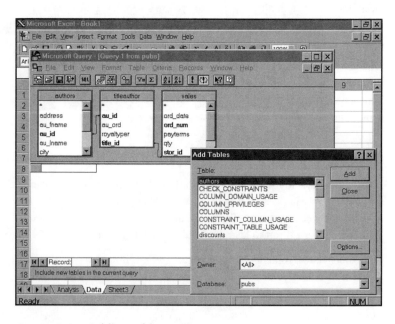

FIGURE 6.1   Adding tables to the query.

4. Click Close on the dialog box.

5. For this exercise, you want the au_fname and au_lname fields from the authors table, and the qty field from the sales table. Double-click each of those fields in order to add them to the query; they'll appear in the grid below the tables as you add them.

6. Click the close box on the MS Query window to dismiss it and return to Excel.

7. Excel will ask you where you want the data to go; put it at R1C1 (row 1, column 1) of the Data sheet.

You now have the data from the database in Excel. But that was too easy! Click somewhere in the data you inserted, and then click the leftmost icon on the External Data toolbar, Edit Query. This takes you back to MS Query.

In the query window, click the toolbar button labeled SQL. A dialog box showing the SQL statement opens (see Figure 6.2), and you can modify the statement directly. Yours should look something like Listing 6.1.

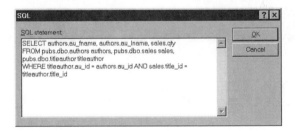

FIGURE 6.2   Editing the SQL statement in MS Query.

LISTING 6.1   SQL from MS Query

```
SELECT authors.au_fname, authors.au_lname, sales.qty
FROM pubs.dbo.authors authors, pubs.dbo.sales sales, ➥
     pubs.dbo.titleauthor titleauthor
WHERE titleauthor.au_id = authors.au_id ➥
  AND sales.title_id = titleauthor.title_id
```

> **Tip**   Looking at the SQL created by MS Query, you
> might notice that it uses the older syntax for the table
> joins. As you will see next, you can still use ANSI JOIN
> syntax because of the way ODBC handles queries.

This capability will be more useful to you when you get into more
complex queries in Lesson 12, "Analyzing Your Data with SQL," but there
are a couple of things you can do now. Because there are authors that will
not have any sales, just as there were authors without titles in Lesson 2,
"Understanding Databases," you should change the SQL to use outer
joins. This will require further changes I will discuss after the code.

Change the SQL to that shown in Listing 6.2. Be sure to type it exactly
as I have shown you. After you have changed it, click OK to close the
dialog.

Listing 6.2   SQL from MS Query

```
SELECT authors.au_fname+' '+authors.au_lname AS name,
       ISNULL( sales.qty, 0 ) AS qty
FROM pubs.dbo.authors authors
LEFT OUTER JOIN titleauthor
ON  titleauthor.au_id = authors.au_id
LEFT OUTER JOIN sales ON sales.title_id = titleauthor.title_id
```

When you press OK, MS Query complains that it can't represent the
query graphically. This just means that it can't show the graphics in the
upper half of the query window if the query is more complex than simple
joins; click OK to continue. The number of rows is much larger now, and
includes the authors who haven't sold books. So what did you do?

You should take notice of three things. First, you told SQL Server to add
the first and last names together, using the plus sign to connect them in
the first part of the SELECT list. Using the plus sign between two character
columns tells SQL Server to *concatenate* the columns. The added space in
single quotes in the middle of the two strings puts a space in between the
names in the output.

Concatenate   Derived from the Latin word for *chain*, concatenation links several objects together to make one composite object. When you concatenate two character columns from the database, you add one directly onto the end of another to create a new character value. For example, concatenating *Smith* and *Jones* creates *SmithJones* for the new value; the example query adds a space in the middle to separate the names.

Adding AS name after a columnref or expression tells SQL Server what to name the column in the results; without this, your calculated columns wouldn't have names. You can use this method to label even single columns, but it is necessary here to use the data effectively in Excel. This technique is called *aliasing*.

Aliasing   Sometimes SQL Server can't assign a name to a column in a result set, so it is up to you to do so. You tell SQL Server what name to use by following the columnref or expression with the name to use. You can use the AS delimiter to set it off from the expression, but it's usually not necessary. The name you assign this way is called the *alias*.

You can also alias table names in the FROM and JOIN parts of your query, as MS Query does in the example.

The last new item is the call to ISNULL() in the last column (it also is aliased, with AS qty). I've added outer joins to retrieve all authors, not just those with sales. If you remember from Lesson 2, this means that some of the rows will have NULL in the right columns because there is no data to return. The ISNULL() function takes two parameters: a columnref and a default value. If the column named in the columnref has a value, that value will be in the row; if it is NULL, ISNULL() replaces the NULL value with the default you supply. In this case, I know that a NULL means there were no sales, so I should send a zero back to Excel.

Close MS Query and continue.

Using the Results

Now that you have the table in Excel, you can use it as you would any other data. If it gets out of date, you can click the red exclamation mark on the External Data toolbar to refresh it. You can also specify when it should be re-queried in the External Data Range Properties dialog (choose it from the context menu invoked by right-clicking on the data).

For an example, extract the data into a graph that shows authors' sales totals. You'll need to define a PivotTable to summarize the data, and then create a chart from it.

1. Click in the data from the database and choose Data, PivotTable Report from the Excel main menu.

2. On page one of the PivotTable Wizard, choose the first item, Microsoft Excel list or database. Click Next.

3. If you clicked in the data before you started the Wizard, the data range is already highlighted in step 2. Click Next.

4. Step 3 asks you to tell Excel how to construct the summaries in the PivotTable. Drag the name box onto the left-hand box labeled ROW, and drag the qty box into the DATA box in the center. This tells Excel to make a row for each name, and then sum up the qtys that have that name in the source table. Figure 6.3 shows the data laid out and ready to go. Click Next.

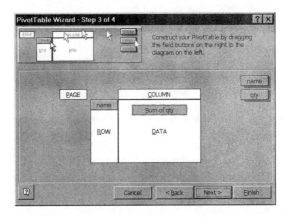

FIGURE 6.3   Setting the data layout for the PivotTable.

5. Choose the Existing worksheet option in the step 4 dialog, and Excel will ask where to put the data. Type Data!R1C5: in the edit box and click Finish. Your finished spreadsheet should look like Figure 6.4.

	1	2	3	4	5	6	7	8	9
1	name	qty			Sum of qty		External Data		
2	Abraham Bennet	5			name	Total			
3	Abraham Bennet	10			Abraham Bennet	15			
4	Reginald Blotchet-Halls	20			Akiko Yokomoto	20			
5	Cheryl Carson	30			Albert Ringer	133			
6	Michel DeFrance	25			Ann Dull	50			
7	Michel DeFrance	15			Anne Ringer	148			
8	Innes del Castillo	10			Burt Gringlesby	20			
9	Ann Dull	50			Charlene Locksley	25			
10	Marjorie Green	5			Cheryl Carson	30	PivotTable		
11	Marjorie Green	10			Dean Straight	15			
12	Marjorie Green	35			Innes del Castillo	10			
13	Morningstar Greene	0			Johnson White	15			
14	Burt Gringlesby	20			Livia Karsen	20			
15	Sheryl Hunter	50			Marjorie Green	50			
16	Smith Jones	0			Michael O'Leary	45			
17	Livia Karsen	20			Michel DeFrance	40			
18	Charlene Locksley	0			Reginald Blotchet-Halls	20			

FIGURE 6.4   Data extracted into a PivotTable.

Now that you have the data summary in your Data sheet, you can proceed to make a chart from it with the following steps:

1. Click in the Sum of Qty cell at the top of the PivotTable you created in the last step, and choose Insert, Chart from Excel's main menu.

2. In step 1 of the Chart Wizard leave the chart as a Column and click Next, and then click Next again on the second step.

3. On the third step, you should probably turn off the legend. (Because you're taking all the authors as a single series, it doesn't help anything.) If you want titles on the chart you can set them here, too, as in Figure 6.5. When you're finished making changes, click Next.

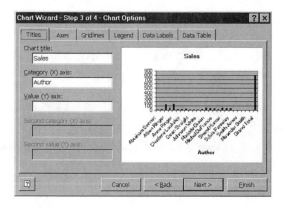

FIGURE 6.5   Setting options in Chart Wizard.

4. Step 4 asks you where to put the chart. Place the chart as an object in your Analysis sheet.

Figure 6.6 shows a chart created this way. On a chart with this many items, you might have to reduce the font size on the legends to see all the authors, so be careful. To see the individual amounts more clearly, you can trim the source data to leave out the Grand Total row from the chart, as I have in Figure 6.6.

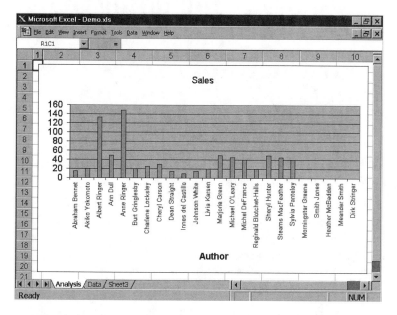

FIGURE 6.6   Data from SQL Server, Charted in Microsoft Excel.

Summary

Using databases is supposed to be harder than this, isn't it? If you have been using Excel to analyze data on your computer, you can see the potential you will gain when you open up your database information to the numerical capabilities in Excel—charting the data is only the start. This lesson showed you the basics of working with data in Excel, and introduced column aliasing and concatenation in SQL.

In the next lesson, you'll finish your tour Office with Microsoft Access. This little database can be a great tool for quick reports from SQL Server data, and with its friendly interface, a real time-saver.

LESSON 7

Including SQL Server Data in Your Microsoft Access Database

In this lesson, you'll learn to use SQL Server tables in Access as if they were part of an Access database.

There are a lot of things to like about SQL Server; you get a lot in the package. However, it is in no danger of being called simple! SQL Server and its supporting programs generally require a large amount of knowledge—some of which you are acquiring now—to use effectively. Access 97 can help, both because it is comparatively simple to use and because it is familiar to many users of desktop systems.

On its own Access 97 is reasonably useful, but its real strength is its capability to pull together data from both desktop and server databases. Systems programmers can use SQL Server to build distributed database solutions across your business (and literally around the world); Access 97 lets you build simple ones right on your desktop. After you connect your Access database to data in SQL Server, you have access (sorry, I had to) to all the user-friendly querying and reporting features you're accustomed to in your desktop databases.

Linking Tables

Access's capabilities come from a simple feature: Within an Access database, you can link tables from ODBC data sources into the Access database, and thereafter treat them as if the data was stored there on your desktop. This is the easiest method of integrating databases from different vendors you'll ever see.

Start Access so you can try this out. Either create a new database to experiment with or open one you don't mind changing.

1. In the database palette (the window with the name of your database at the top), click the **New** button, and then choose **Link-table** and click **OK**.

2. The Link dialog (see Figure 7.1) looks a lot like a normal Office 97 file opening box, but it has a quirk: On the **Files of type:** list, scroll all the way to the bottom and choose **ODBC Databases()**. The file dialog box disappears, to be replaced with the ODBC Data Source window you've used before.

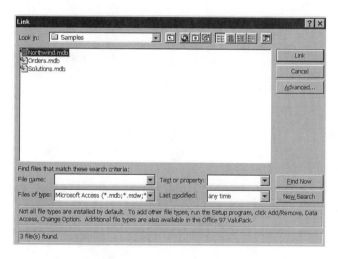

FIGURE 7.1   Linking tables in Access 97.

3. You can choose either a file or traditional registry-based DSN; choose the pubs data source we've been using.

4. Log in to the database if you need to, and you're presented with a list of all the tables in the pubs database. Select your old friends **authors, titleauthor,** and **titles** from the list by clicking them. Click **OK** and you're done.

After a little delay, you see the tables in the list of tables in your database window, as in Figure 7.2. You can recognize the linked tables by the "world" icon next to their names, instead of the grid icon that identifies local tables. Notice also that, instead of leaving the names as they are in the source database, Access names them with the owner's alias (dbo), an underscore, and the table name. You'll have to rename them to use the same SQL on the server and in Access.

FIGURE 7.2 Linked tables showing in the Database palette.

You can update linked tables, but you might experience conflicts with other users of the server because of the way data is copied back and forth between Access and SQL Server. If you decide to modify data in Access through linked tables, you should plan ahead to minimize contention with other users.

Tip   My comments about updating linked tables aside, Access is a very good application for moving data across heterogeneous databases. If, for example, you link tables to a source database in Oracle and a target in SQL Server, it's trivial to copy the data with the INSERT...SELECT syntax you saw in Lesson 4, "Adding and Changing Data." Performance is unexciting, and the Data Transformation Services in SQL Server 7 supply similar functionality, but Access is always available for quick transfers.

There are other issues at work in using this feature. The simplicity you see on the surface comes at a very real cost in complexity under the hood. For the uses you see here, you should have no problem, but if you decide to build applications in Access 97 based on SQL Server tables, be sure to read the online documentation before you proceed with your design.

The immediate benefit you'll gain from linked tables will be in using the data with Access's tools for querying and reporting.

Using Access for Reporting

Other, more feature-filled report writers exist. If you have one available and have learned how to use it, you probably should. On the other hand, Access can produce good, simple reports without requiring you to purchase any more software or undergo further training.

You should construct any report in three steps. The first, deciding what you need, seems obvious, but you might need to look at it closely. You can find yourself flailing trying to create a report, particularly one for someone else, if you don't plan out up front what you're going to do.

On this report, I want the basic name, address, and phone information, arranged in a tabular format. You'll create a tabular directory of authors that people can take in their briefcases, in case they need to get in touch with an author while away from the office.

The second and third steps are to create a query to retrieve the data, and then build the report based on that data. I prefer to build reports based on separate queries to keep the data separate from the layout and formatting in the report, although you can build a reasonable report direct from tables using the grouping and sorting features of the report generator. I've found it is much easier to keep things separate, though, in case you need to change the retrieval later.

Defining the Query

For this report, you only need the authors' names, addresses, and phone numbers from the authors table. Follow these steps to create the query:

1. Switch to the **Queries** tab in the database window and click **New**.

2. Choose **Design View** and click **OK**.

3. Add the dbo_authors table in the following dialog, and then
close it.

4. You're left at the query design window in Access. In the preceding
table, double-click on these fields in order to add them to the
query: **au_fname**, **au_lname**, **phone**, **address**, **city**, **state**, and
zip. The finished query should look like that shown in Figure 7.3.

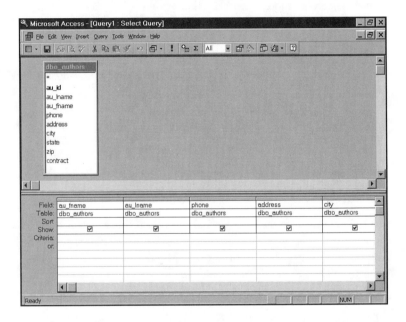

FIGURE 7.3   Querying the authors database in SQL Server through
Access 97.

If you look at the data sheet view (click the icon in the toolbar), you'll see
that the results aren't sorted as you might prefer. You can change this by
setting the **Sort** line under the column you'd prefer to sort by, or you can
take care of this later in the report building stage. The same SQL goes to
the server regardless.

When you're done with the query, save it and continue to the **Reports** tab.

Building the Report

In the last step, you will build the report itself. Because you have simple output to create, you'll use the tabular AutoReport to build it.

Follow these steps:

1. On the **Reports** tab, click the **New** button.

2. The dialog that appears presents you with a list of reports that you can create.

3. From the dialog, choose **AutoReport: Tabular** from the list, and then select the name of your query from the drop-down below it and click **OK**.

Access crunches for a little, and then up pops a report listing the data from the address query, formatted and ready to customize (see Figure 7.4). I'll usually change at least the column names in a report generated by Access, because it always uses the column names from the table—rarely what you want in a printed work.

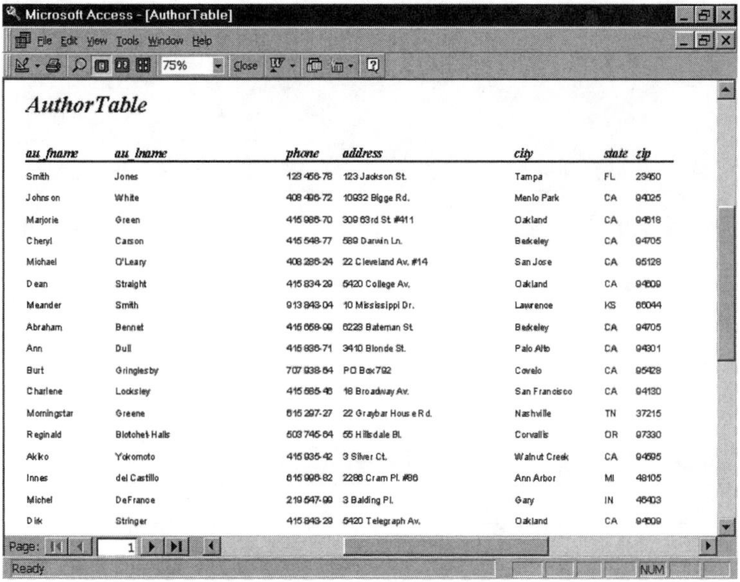

FIGURE 7.4   The generated report in Access 97.

After you have created the report, you might modify it in Design view to change fields, add text and graphics, change the sort order, and so forth. In the Design view of the generated report, there are four panes containing data and the toolbar as in Figure 7.5. You can use graphics, controls, and implements from the toolbar by clicking the appropriate element and dragging it out on the screen. The field properties window (titled Text Box: phone in Figure 7.5) sets the data source for a data field you create this way. I'll show you how to use this when I discuss the Detail pane.

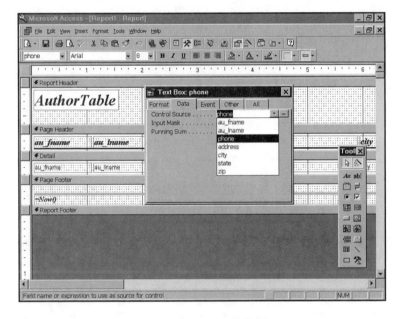

FIGURE 7.5   The data source for a Detail field.

The number of panes that show in the report design will vary with the type of report you create. In this report, you have the items in Table 7.1.

TABLE 7.1   Report Format Panes in the Tabular Report

Pane	Layout Element
Report Header	Printed once at the start of the report
Page Header	Printed at the top of each page

Pane	Layout Element
Detail	Lays out the fields in each detail row of the report
Page Footer	Printed at the bottom of each page
Report Footer	Printed once at the end of the report

The header and footer panes are self explanatory. The Detail pane is the only one that isn't immediately obvious. This pane, rather than passing through literal text (or a simple Access 97 function like Now( )), takes the values of the fields in each row of the query and lays them out. Instead of being literal text, the information in each box is the name of the field it will receive from the row. To see this, perform the following steps:

1. Right-click one of the dotted boxes in the Detail pane.

2. Click **Properties** on the context menu.

3. In the properties dialog that opens, click the **Data** tab. You'll see the field name, as shown in Figure 7.5.

I've clicked the drop-down to show you that you can specify any field in the query to go into this box in the Detail portion of the report.

There are a couple of quick things you can do to make the report look a little better. First, edit the text in the Page Header to be a little friendlier; for example, click on **au_fname** (the one in bold italic), erase the current text with the **Backspace** key, and then type First name. More people will know what that means. Change the other legends to titles that appeal to you (I'd change the report title in the report header, too).

Second, because the authors' last names are nowhere near as large as the boxes allocated to them, narrow the box some. Click on the **au_lname** box in the detail pane; notice the boxes that appear on its border. If you grab a box with the mouse (click and drag with the primary button), you'll move the corresponding corner or edge. So narrow the **au_lname** box by dragging the box in the center of the right-hand edge in to about half its original width.

Because the other fields are left hanging out to the right, drag their boxes in close where they should be by dragging their boxes to the left (don't click on them first). You'll have to line up the columns in the header to match, of course. Experiment a little, and switch back to layout view by clicking the **View** icon on the toolbar to see your results. Mine is shown in Figure 7.6.

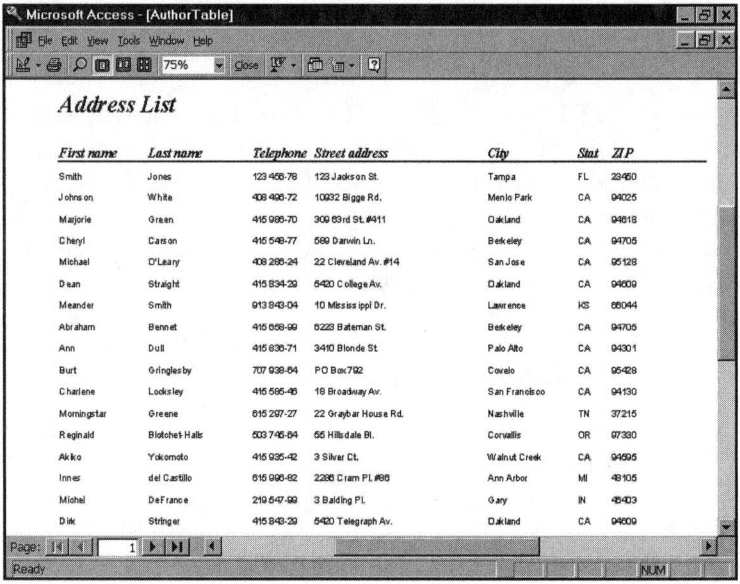

Figure 7.6   My finished report in Access 97.

I can't take you through all there is to laying out reports in Access 97. If what you've seen appeals to you, take a minute to experiment with different kinds of reports and queries before you go on. Try using the query you've been using to retrieve authors and their titles, and then build a report to print an index of authors to publications.

Summary

In this lesson, you saw how easy it is to create great-looking reports in Access 97 without a lot of effort. Much more complex reporting is possible, with a little ingenuity applied to the query and layout.

Before you could use Access to create reports from SQL Server, though, you had to learn another important capability: using linked tables in Access to gain access to remote data sources from a local desktop database. Whenever I'm working heavily with databases, I always end up learning a new use for this feature. I expect you'll find it useful, as well.

That's it for the desktop application-oriented lessons. In the next few lessons, you'll learn how to build applications that take SQL Server data to the Web.

LESSON 8
Simple Web Publishing

In this lesson, you'll learn to create a dynamic Web site with SQL Server and the Internet Data Connector.

You should be able to satisfy most of your database needs at your desk now. I've covered database structure, basic SQL statements, and using SQL Server data in Microsoft Office. That will take care of what you need for using databases day to day, but I'll wager that you don't work in isolation— you have to be able to provide information to others. Now, you'll extend your reach to providing that information on your *intranet*.

 Intranet Out in the great big world is the Internet, a global Gordian Net of computer connectivity. Rather than expose their data to the Internet, most companies implement an intranet, an internal network that connects just the servers and users within the company. An intranet might have a connection to the Internet so employees can use it, but it usually keeps Internet users out with a security device like a firewall.

It appears these days that no network application is going anywhere now if it isn't on the Web. There are some good reasons for this, not least of which is that with care (and plenty of testing) you can distribute information and applications with a Web server to anyone on any platform. This *platform independence* can mean real savings in support costs for intranet applications. It solves a tricky problem that I know you've encountered: You need to give a document to someone else to look at electronically, but he doesn't have your word processing program, or you're on a PC and he's on a Mac, or… The problem is that you have one *platform*—the combination of your computer, operating system, and software applications—and others might have completely different setups.

Platform Independent Platform independent refers to applications that can run on any of a large group of different platforms without modification. The Web promises this sort of freedom, and delivers to some degree, but in practice you must test applications on all the platforms your users will work on.

Despite its advantages, the Web has its drawbacks. Web technology evolves at a frustratingly frenetic pace; no sooner are you adjusted to the current state-of-the-art than someone comes out with another technology that supposedly you *must* use. Just say no. I'm going to stick with HTML only here because corporate network policies often outlaw even widely accepted technologies like Java. Your mileage might vary, but my experience has been that the technology mix most likely to succeed in everyone's intranet is HTML with perhaps JavaScript.

In this lesson you're going to learn to use Microsoft's Internet Database Connector (IDC) to build database applications. Sites built using IDC can be deployed on everything from a laptop computer running Personal Web Server (PWS) to huge megasites running NT Server and Internet Information Server (IIS). You don't *need* any additional development tools to build IDC sites—you can get by just fine with Notepad. I usually use a Web page editor to lay out the page and then add in the database code, but it's not strictly necessary.

 Caution This is not the place to learn Web page development. I can show you some specific techniques, but overall I have to assume you know how to build basic Web pages. The good news is you don't have to be an HTML wizard; if you have built a "home page" or two for yourself, you should be fine.

You won't require a huge server for these lessons; I double-check the examples on a fairly powerful NT server, but I built most of them on a laptop running Windows 98, SQL Server 7, and PWS. If you don't already have an IIS server available, the easiest thing for you is probably to install PWS on your desktop. You'll also need to connect a DSN *on the Web server* to the Northwind database on your SQL Server. Follow the steps you used in Lesson 5 to create pubs, but name your new data source "nwind7" in step 3, and change to the Northwind database in step 5.

> **Caution**   You have to set up the data source on the Web server, not on your client computer! If you are developing on the same computer the Web server is running on, it won't matter, but if not, setting the data source up on your computer won't do you a bit of good. The IDC files are processed on the server, so the data source has to be set up on that computer, not your client.

How It Works

IDC is part of Microsoft's IIS and PWS (for Windows NT and Windows 95/98, respectively). It is one of the oldest and most stable of the features in IIS; my printed copy of the IIS 2.0 documentation (circa 1996) has essentially the same information on IDC as that in the IIS 4.0 server the examples in this chapter were built on.

IDC creates Web pages dynamically from database data using a template you specify as shown in Figure 8.1. In the figure, the upper side reflects the incoming request, whereas the lower side follows the response returning to the user.

The user agent, usually a Web browser, sends a Hypertext Transfer Protocol (HTTP) request to the Web server specifying the IDC file as the target. IIS invokes the HTTPODBC dynamic link library (DLL), which contains the processing code for IDC. IDC reads the .idc file to retrieve the database connection information and whatever queries it is supposed to execute. After filling in any replacement parameters in the .idc file (I'll get to that), it sends the queries to the ODBC data source specified in the file.

When IDC gets the request back from the database, it reads the .htx file to format the response to the user. The .htx file is a Hypertext Markup Language (HTML) file containing special tags that IDC will replace with data from the database queries. IDC hands the completed page to IIS, which handles the protocol requirements to return the response to the user's browser.

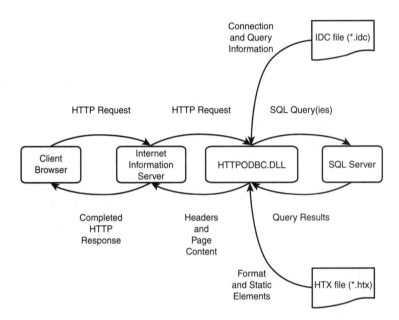

FIGURE 8.1 Internet Database Connector Structure.

 Tip For further information on the Internet Database connector, look in the Microsoft Developer Network (MSDN) Library, either on CD or at msdn.microsoft.com. It's hidden away under **Platform SDK, Internet/Intranet/Extranet-Services, Internet Information Services SDK, Reference, Internet Database Connector.**

The IDC File

The IDC file specifies at least three elements: the ODBC data source, a query to run on the data source, and the name of the file to read formatting information from (the HTX file). You can also supply additional information, including database login and password. Each element in the IDC contains the name of the element, a colon, and the data for the element. The entries you must include in the IDC file are listed in Table 8.1 and optional entries are in Table 8.2.

TABLE 8.1 Required IDC Data Elements

Element	Purpose
Datasource: *dsn*	Specifies the data source; *dsn* is the name of an ODBC DSN on the Web server
SQLStatement: *sql*	Holds the query to run on the data source; *sql* can be spread across several lines, if you place a '+' at the beginning of the second and subsequent lines
Template: *htxfile*	Names the template file that will be used to format the response to the user

TABLE 8.2 Common Optional IDC Data Elements

Element	Purpose
Username: *userid*	Database login to use
Password: *pw*	Database password to use
Expires: *seconds*	Tells the client to reload the page from the server if its cached copy is older than *seconds*
RequiredParameters: *parm* [, *parm* ...]	Parameters that must be supplied in the HTTP request from the client; IDC will return an error if they aren't there
MaxRecords: *n*	Tells IDC to process at most *n* records from the query results

Listing 8.1 shows a basic IDC file that logs in to the nwind7 DSN to retrieve an employee list.

LISTING 8.1   EmpIndex.idc Retrieves Employees from Northwind

```
Datasource: nwind7
Username: sa
Template: empIndex.htx
SQLStatement: SELECT LastName + ', ' + FirstName as EName,
+   EmployeeID, Title
+ FROM Employees
+ ORDER BY LastName, FirstName
```

If you look at the SQL in Listing 8.1, you see I've used a new feature of SQL without describing it first: ORDER BY is too useful not to introduce, though, and this example needs it. You use ORDER BY after the FROM in your SELECT to tell SQL Server to sort the output. Just list the columns in the order you want the output sorted. The example sorts by the last name, and then, if more than one person has the same last name, by first name, too.

Store this in a file on your Web server named EmpIndex.idc; make sure it's in a directory with scripting permissions turned on (check with your system administrator if you need help). Next, you'll create a template file to format the output.

The HTX File

The HTX file (*.htx) is the output side of the IDC. The HTX file contains standard HTML plus tags, marked with server script delimiters (<% ... %>) that are replaced with data values or executed as commands when the page is created to send back to the user. Listing 8.2 shows the template file for the employee page.

LISTING 8.2   EmpIndex.htx Formats the Employee Index

```
1: <html>
2: <head>
3: <title>Northwind Employees</title>
4: </head>
5: <body>
6: <h1><em>Employee List</em></h1>
7: <hr>
8: <table>
9:     <% ' database oriented stuff; this section prints the
```

continues

Listing 8.2   Continued

```
10:            ' table header on the first time through, then the
11:            ' row of data on that and subsequent iterations.
12:     %>
13:     <%begindetail%>
14:         <%if CurrentRecord EQ 0%>
15:             <tr>
16:                 <td>
17:                     <h3>Employee</h3>
18:                 </td>
19:                 <td>
20:                     <h3>Position</h3>
21:                 </td>
22:             </tr>
23:         <%endif%>
24:         <tr>
25:             <td>
26:                 <A HREF=➧
27: "employee.idc?EmployeeID=<%EmployeeID%>"><%EName%></A>
28:             </td>
29:             <td>
30:                 <em><%title%></em>
31:             </td>
32:         </tr>
33:     <%enddetail%>
34: </table>
35: </body>
36: </html>
```

Type this in a text file named EmpIndex.htx in the same directory as the
IDC file. Because Windows filenames aren't case-sensitive, you can use
any capitalization you like, but it's good form to be consistent.

> **Tip**   Take note of the formatting in the examples. If
> you format your scripts and HTML using a standard
> layout, it makes it a lot easier to go back and make
> changes or fix bugs, and can help keep bugs out in
> the first place.

After you've created the file, open your browser and connect to
http://*yourservername*/*pathtoyourdirectory*/empIndex.idc, in which
yourservername is the name of your Web server and *pathtoyourdirectory*

is the directory in which you stored the IDC and HTX files. The path is usually a relative path from the server's `inetpub\wwwroot` directory.

When you connect to the page, you'll see something like Figure 8.2.

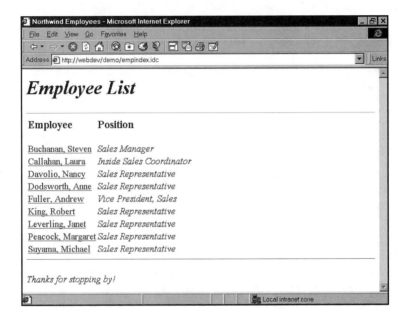

FIGURE 8.2   Employee Index from IDC.

IDC is going to ignore everything in the HTX file that isn't inside script delimiters; the rest just gets sent to the client as HTML. I'll refer to sections of the text set off this way as *script blocks*. The following paragraphs discuss the script in Listing 8.2.

Comments

The first script block, lines 9 to 12, is only comments. Within a block, you can use the single apostrophe to tell IDC to ignore anything following it on the line; this is important as your scripts get more complicated in order to remind you what you were trying to accomplish. You can include comments with the HTML syntax, but if you use a script block, they are not sent out to the browser.

Query Output

The next script block uses the IDC keywords begindetail (line 13)and
enddetail (line 33) to tell IDC that this is where it is going to put the data
from the query. The HTML between these tags will be sent to the client
once for every row returned by the query. To include a field from the row
in the output, you include a script block that contains only the field name,
as in lines 27 and 30. There are three fields output here, EmployeeID, EName
(the concatenated last name and first name of the employee from the SQL
in the IDC file), and title, the employee's position.

Decisions, Decisions...

The next script block (lines 14 to 23) shows an additional feature of IDC;
within the HTX file you can make decisions with this construct:

```
<%if expression%>
    send this HTML to the client
<%else%>
    send this HTML to the client, instead
<%endif%>
```

In this statement, the *expression* is a statement that is either true or false;
if it is true, the HTML and script after the <%if ... %> is sent to the
output; otherwise, if an <%else%> is present, the HTML after it is used.
The <%endif%> must be present to end the statement. In the example, the
statement checks the CurrentRecord variable to see if the detail section is
being executed for the first time, and if so, it prints out the header row of
the table. Table 8.3 lists the operators you can use in the expression you're
checking, and Table 8.4 shows the values that IDC gives you.

TABLE 8.3   IDC Operators

Operator	Purpose
EQ	True if parameters are equal
LT	True if the left parameter is less than the right
GT	True if the left parameter is greater than the right
CONTAINS	For text data; true if the left parameter has the right parameter in it anywhere

TABLE 8.4   IDC-Supplied Values

Name	Value
CurrentRecord	Number of times the begindetail/ enddetail block has been sent out
MaxRecords	Value specified in the IDC file

You can also use HTTP or request variables. To use HTTP variables, preface the name of the variable with "HTTP_," capitalize all letters, and change all dashes to underscores; Content-Type becomes HTTP_CONTENT_TYPE.

To use variables from the URL or request form, use the syntax idc.*variablename*. The next example, Listing 8.3, shows this.

 Tip   SQL Server includes a feature called the Web Assistant Wizard to generate pages from databases using a template file similar to an IDC HTX file. Its limitation is that it only generates static HTML from the database; it does not support the interaction with the data that IDC and ASP do, so I don't go into it here. For more information, please see SQL Server Books Online.

Using Parameters

The first example included an anchor around the employee's name, that invoked another IDC file with a parameter, EmployeeID. Listing 8.3 shows employee.idc and employee.htx, that retrieve and display the employee information.

LISTING 8.3   Retrieving Employee Data

```
1: <ic:input>
2:
3: (employee.idc)
4:
```

continues

LISTING 8.3   Continued

```
 5: datasource: nwind7
 6: username: sa
 7: template: employee.htx
 8: maxFieldSize: 4096
 9: SQLStatement:
10: + SELECT e.TitleOfCourtesy cTitle,
11: +          e.FirstName + ' ' + e.LastName ename,
12: +          boss.FirstName + ' ' + boss.LastName bossName,
13: +          boss.EmployeeID AS bossID,
14: +          e.Title title,
15: +          convert(varchar(10), e.BirthDate, 101) bday,
16: +          convert(varchar(10), e.HireDate, 101) hday,
17: +          e.Extension extension,
18: +          convert( varchar(5000), e.notes ) notes
19: + FROM Employees e
20: + LEFT OUTER JOIN Employees boss
21: +                 ON boss.EmployeeID = e.ReportsTo
22: + WHERE   e.EmployeeID = %EmployeeID%
23:
24: (employee.htx)
25:
26: <html>
27: <head>
28: <title>Employee datasheet</title>
29: </head>
30: <body>
31: <%begindetail%>
32: <h1>Employee information for <%ctitle%> <%ename%></h1>
33: <hr>
34: Employee ID: <%idc.EmployeeID%><br>
35: Position: <%title%><br>
36: Hired on: <%hday%><br>
37: Phone : x<%extension%><br>
38: Supervisor:
39:     <A HREF="employee.idc?EmployeeID=<%bossID%>">
40:         <%bossName%>
41:     </A><br>
42: Notes:<br>
43: <em><%notes%></em><br>
44: <hr>
45: <A HREF="empIndex.idc">Return</A> to the employee index.
46: <%enddetail%>
47: </body>
48: </html>
```

If you place these files in the same directory with the index page, you'll see the page in Figure 8.3 when you choose an employee.

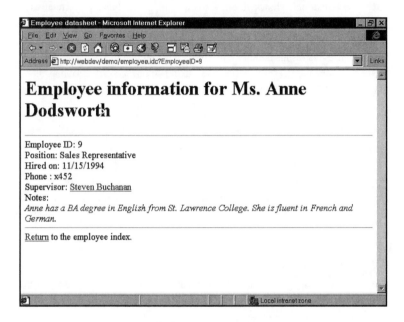

FIGURE 8.3   Employee Information from IDC.

Each of the employee names in the index page (lines 26 and 27 in Listing 8.2) has an anchor around it with a URL that looks like `employee.idc?EmployeeID=<%EmployeeID%>`. The part of the URL after the question mark is the parameter list; you can include multiple parameters separated by a comma. In the IDC for this example, the WHERE on line 22 shows how to use the parameter from the URL to pick the employee it displays. If you've worked with forms, you know that this uses the HTTP GET method; you can also use POSTed variables (as you would with forms).

The SQL for this example introduces you to two new things. First, I use the `convert` function for the dates and the `notes` field on lines 15, 16, and 18. For the date fields, I used it to format the date to display the way I wanted to see it. I used it for the `notes` field to force the entire field to be output; by default, you'd only see the first 40 characters from the column.

Second, the Employees table uses a reflexive relation; the ReportsTo column references the EmployeeID of another employee row in the same table. The SQL in the example shows you how to navigate across this type of relation; you have to join the table to itself (lines 20 and 21) in order to tell SQL Server to look at the same table and get the row that matches the ReportsTo id. Because this brings another employee record into your result (now you have two EmployeeID's, two FirstName's, and so on), you have to alias the tables to tell SQL Server which columns you're referring to in the rest of the query.

The HTX file also uses the EmployeeID from the URL, at line 34. This line prints out the id in the manner I told you of earlier, using <%idc.EmployeeID%> to retrieve the value from the URL. You can do quite a bit with this; I'm only showing retrievals, but you can use UPDATE and INSERT in your SQL to update the database based on parameters from a request.

Summary

The examples in this lesson show how easy it is to create database-driven Webs with IDC. With just a few minutes of effort, you've created an employee index for the Web, in Notepad no less!

Building a database page in IDC takes three steps:

1. Create or choose a data source.

2. Build an IDC file that retrieves the data you need.

3. Build an HTX file to display the output.

There could be a fourth step, I suppose: explaining to everyone how you did it so quickly!

IDC is good for applications that don't need a lot of intelligence, like retrievals or form updates to the database. If you need more intelligent processing on the server, you'll have to look at a richer technology. You'll see one of them in the next chapter: Active Server Pages.

LESSON 9

Advanced Web Publishing

This lesson will teach you the basics of using Active Server Pages (ASP) and ActiveX Data Objects (ADO) to create interactive Web applications.

Active Server Pages (ASP) is Microsoft's main glue technology for all server-side processing on Internet Information Server. Internet Data Connector (IDC) was built specifically to hook up databases and Web sites so the data can be retrieved, updated, or otherwise manipulated. With this specific purpose, it is limited in capability otherwise.

ASP, on the other hand, is intended as a general purpose server scripting technology. With ASP and COM-enabled applications, you can design and build server applications to your needs, using whatever architectural pattern you like. I'll show you one way to use SQL Server data in ASP, but this is far from the limit of its capabilities.

COM COM, Microsoft's Component Object Model, is the technological underpinning for most application interaction in Windows. For example, when you choose to embed a PowerPoint graphic into a Word document, Word communicates with PowerPoint through COM facilities. Since a program can access other programs and data items (objects, in COM parlance) through standard interfaces, you can mix and match software from different vendors according to your preferences.

Tip   Until now, I haven't advised you to invest in development tools for building anything. ASP is a powerful tool for building intranet applications (I show it to you because these applications usually include databases like SQL Server). If you plan to build larger sites with ASP, you might be exceeding what I would consider manageable without design and development tools made for building Web applications.

To work effectively in ASP you will need to learn at least a little of a scripting language. The two you will normally have installed are Microsoft's Visual Basic Scripting Edition, or VBScript, and Microsoft's version of JavaScript, JScript. It's simpler in many ways to stick with VBScript when you are learning to build ASP applications, so that is what I will use here.

Note   Unfortunately, a full-fledged tutorial on scripting with VBScript is beyond what I can give you here. I'll explain what I present, but if this is your first exposure to it, I'd advise you to look to the source, at http://microsoft.com/scripting.

ASP is a complex and powerful platform for building Webs. If you don't get the hang of it right away, rest assured you're not alone. Many Web page authors reading this will be seeing ASP for the first time, and it's a little complicated. I am going to show you what you need to create basic ASP scripts using SQL Server, but you might still have questions. If this topic is of interest to you, this lesson could be as much a teaser as instruction! If you get stuck, take a look at the Microsoft MSDN and scripting sites I've mentioned.

How It Works

ASP files, marked with the extension .asp, are programs the Web server executes, usually to create an HTML page to return to the client. ASP pages are built using script blocks in an HTML file, similar to the HTX files you worked with in the last lesson, but there is no IDC file to concern yourself with. When the server sees a request for an .asp file, it loads the file into a script interpreter that reads the file from start to finish. Anything that isn't a script block is sent straight through to the client browser, but when it sees a script block, it compiles and executes any programming commands in the block before moving on. Let's take the whirlwind tour of scripting with VBScript. Consider the ASP in Listing 9.1.

LISTING 9.1   My First Active Server Page

```
<html>
<head>
<title>Y2K Status</title>
</head>
<body>
<br>
<h3>We have
        <%
            if now() < CDate("1/1/2000") then
                Response.Write("not")
            End if
        %>
    passed Y2K.</h3>
<br>
</body>
</html>
```

This script has one script block in it: using the VBScript `if` statement to check `now()`, a function to get the current date and time, against January 1, 2000. (`CDate` changes the `String` date to a VBScript `Date` so I can compare it to `now()`.) If that date hasn't arrived, it prints the "not" in the sentence to let you know it hasn't come yet. After New Year's, it will omit the negative.

> **Note**   Internet Information Server assumes that ASP scripts are written using VBScript if you don't tell it otherwise. If you want to use JScript, you should include the directive `<%@ LANGUAGE=JScript %>` at the beginning of your ASP file.

Variables

You use objects and simple data items with named copies of them called *variables*. At the most basic level, a variable name refers to an area of storage that the computer sets aside to store a single data value like the number 5 or a string like "Hi, how are you?" You'll usually not have to worry about storage, though. You can simply deal with variables in the same way as variables in math (the x in ax + by = c). In VBScript, you can set a variable to a simple value by typing x = 5, or you can calculate a value to store in it, by typing something like x = y + 2.

By default, VBScript will create simple variables on the fly as you use them. This can create bugs that are very hard to see, though, so you can use the statement Option Explicit at the start of your script to disable automatic variables. With this option set, you must use the Dim keyword to *declare* a variable, or tell VBScript about it before you use it. Unlike other variants of Visual Basic, Dim in VBScript only tells VBScript you're going to use a variable, not what type it is. However, since VBScript will give you an error if you use an undeclared variable, this can save you from a lot of typographical errors. I haven't used explicit declarations in this lesson, to keep the examples short, but in Lesson 10, "An Interactive Web Application," I'll show you how Dim is used.

Objects

The most interesting part of Listing 9.1 is how it puts the word into the sentence using the Response object. In VBScript, anything more complicated than a number or a string is an *object*. The Response object holds the HTML that is being sent back to the client. The example tells the Response object to write "not" into the HTML, by saying Response.Write("not"). I've mentioned objects in passing before, but it's time to get into a little more detail.

An object like Response is an *instance* of a *class*. A class, or *object type*, is a description of one kind of object you may use, in terms of the data that objects of that type will have and what you may do with those objects. A simple variable can hold one value internal to your script and only provides simple means for working with that value. An object, on the other hand, can hold several values, and normally has more complicated behavior than simple data items.

When your script is running, you may work with many objects of the same type; each of those specific objects is an object instance, often just called an object. An object in ASP can be a built-in VBScript object like Response, or an instance of a COM class like an ActiveX Data Objects (ADO) Recordset. Built-in objects are described in the VBScript documentation and are always the same. The COM classes available to you depend on what software is installed on your computer and are described in the documentation for the software providing that kind of object. The COM classes installed on your computer are listed in the registry under HKEY_CLASSES_ROOT.

The name you use to refer to an object instance is called an *object variable*. You usually create object variables in ASP to work with something that already exists, like a table in the database. Some object variables you'll often use include the Request that the user's browser sent, the Server your script is running on, and the Response you are sending back to the client. These are so common, in fact, that the VBScript interpreter declares them for you.

VBScript does not create objects automatically the way it does with simple data. You create an object with the Server object's CreateObject method, as in Server.CreateObject("ClassName"), or by calling a method of another existing object, then assigning the result to an object variable. You'll see this later in practice.

To tell an object to do something, you use one of its *methods*, whereas to set or retrieve the data it contains, you use one of its *properties*. To use an object's methods or properties, you write Object.member in your script, where *Object* is the name of the object you want to use, and *member* is either a method or a property.

When you need to give a method additional information about how to do what you're asking, you follow the name of the method with the information values (or variables containing the values). If there are more than one of these *parameters*, separate them with commas. You can surround these values with parentheses when calling a function (which returns a value, as in Sin(1.2)), but in most cases they aren't necessary. I'll include them more often than not, just as a matter of style. Listing 9.1 showed how to use a method on the Response object, by invoking the Write method of the Response object to send the string "not" to the output.

Statements

You get your work done in VBScript mostly by manipulating objects with *statements*, the third important part of scripting. A statement, such as the `if...then...end if` I used to check the date in Listing 9.1, is a single instruction to the computer to take an action or make a decision. You can use VBScript to write script files to execute at a DOS prompt in Windows, for macros in Office applications, or for ASP on a Web site; the objects you can manipulate are different in each case, but by and large the statements are the same.

You've already seen the `if` statement. Another one you will use over and over is the *assignment*, which sets the value of an object or an object property. To *assign* a value to an item, you write the target's name, the equals sign, and then the value or object that you want the target to hold. To set an integer variable named x to the value 5, you write x = 5. For object variables, you need to use the `Set` keyword before the assignment, as in `Set objX = objY`. Unfortunately, you can sometimes assign objects without `Set` because VBScript won't complain, but your application might fail in mysterious ways later. Test well, and use `Set`.

The last statement I'll look at is the `while` statement. Its syntax is as follows:

```
while condition
    statement
    [statement ...]
wend
```

In the `while`, *condition* is a formula that is either true or false; as long as the condition is true, the statement(s) between the `while` line and the `wend` are executed over and over in a *loop*. After the condition becomes false, the script interpreter moves on to the next statement after the `wend`. Yes, if you're following along, this means that one of the statements inside the loop has to change something the condition is based on or the script will never stop looping; this condition, called an *infinite loop*, has never happened in my code, but I've heard of it.

That's the VBScript prep course. There's a lot more to the language, but I think you've covered enough to go on to ActiveX Data Objects (ADO).

ActiveX Data Objects

ADO is the future of data access on Microsoft platforms. At present, it is still dependent on the ODBC interfaces I've been using, so I'll still be connecting with ODBC DSNs. With ADO, you'll work with Connections to databases and Recordsets that you retrieve from them.

Within ADO, a Connection is the object class you use to handle connecting to and logging in to the database. You ask the server to create an object of type ADODB.Connection, and then tell the object to connect to a database using the connection information you supply. If all goes well, you can then work with the data in the database.

After you've connected, you can retrieve data from the Connection into an ADODB.Recordset, which is used to look at rows returned from a query you send to the database. The Recordset object can work with data from a SELECT or a table as a whole. You can update or insert data in a table or simple SELECT, but not from a query that retrieves from more than one table.

When you retrieve data with a Recordset, it acts as a view of a row of the data you're looking at. You can change which row it gives you information from using its MovePrev, MoveNext, MoveFirst, and MoveLast methods, among others. To scan through the records in a Recordset, you first retrieve the data, and then move forward to each row in turn with MoveNext until the Eof property becomes true. This property, named for historical reasons for an end-of-file condition, becomes true when you move past the last row in the Recordset.

That'll do for background. I'm going to gradually introduce more of VBScript, so you'll pick it up as you go forward. Next, you'll see an example to show you how these things work together, and then in the next lesson, you'll get even more as you build a complete application with ASP.

Displaying Data

For this lesson's examples, I'll show you how to build the employee index you built in the last lesson, but you'll implement it with ASP and ADO this time. To run these programs, you'll need to have IIS or PWS again, and the nwind7 data source configured on the Web server.

The first example, EmpIndex.asp, is shown in Listing 9.2 and Figure 9.1.

LISTING 9.2   Employee Index in ASP: EmpIndex.asp

```
 1: <% Response.Expires = 0 %>
 2: <HTML>
 3: <HEAD>
 4: <title>Northwind Employees</title>
 5: </HEAD>
 6: <BODY>
 7: <OBJECT RUNAT=server PROGID=ADODB.Connection
 8:           id=EmployeeConn> </OBJECT>
 9: <P>
10: <%
11:     EmployeeConn.Open( "DSN=nwind7;UID=sa" )
12:     set rs = EmployeeConn.Execute(
13:               "SELECT LastName + ', ' + FirstName " +_
14:               "AS EName, EmployeeID, Title " +_
15:               "FROM Employees " +_
16:               "ORDER BY LastName, FirstName, Title" )
17:     if not rs.Eof then
18:     %>
19:     <h1><em>Employee List</em></h1>
20:     <hr>
21:         <table>
22:             <tr>
23:                 <td>
24:                     <h3>Employee</h3>
25:                 </td>
26:                 <td>
27:                     <h3>Position</h3>
28:                 </td>
29:             </tr>
30:
31:             <%
32:             while not rs.Eof
33:             %>
34:                 <tr>
35:                     <td>
36:                       <A HREF="Employee.asp?EmployeeID=
37:                             <%=rs("EmployeeID")%>">
38:                             <%=rs("EName")%></A>
39:                     </td>
40:                     <td>
41:                         <em><%=rs("title")%></em>
42:                     </td>
43:                 </tr>
```

```
44:                    <%
45:                        rs.MoveNext
46:                wend
47:            %>
48:            </table>
49:        <hr>
50:        <br>
51:        <em>Thanks for stopping by!</em>
52:        <br>
53: <%
54:        end if
55: %>
56: </BODY>
57: </HTML>
```

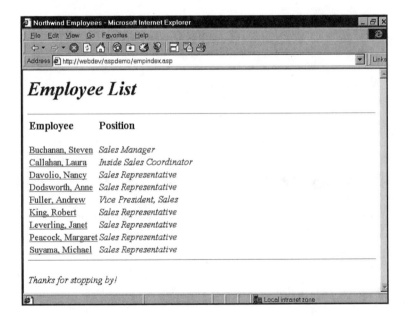

Figure 9.1 Employee Index from ASP.

Yes, it looks like a lot, but it's really not. Take it one step at a time, the way that the ASP script interpreter does, by looking at each line of the listing in order. Because ASP will send the normal HTML to the client without processing it, I'm going to skip over them and just discuss the script blocks, set off as usual by the script delimiters <% and %>.

The first script block, Response.Expires = 0 (at line 1), sets the Response object's Expires property to zero seconds. This tells the client not to cache a copy of the page. I'll commonly use this to force the browser to retrieve the latest data from the server instead of relying on a local copy.

The next not-normal-HTML line is the OBJECT tag at line 7; the OBJECT HTML tag was originally created to use ActiveX controls or Java applets in the page on the client computer. With the RUNAT=server parameter, though, it creates the object on the server, instead; in this case, it's an ADO Connection object named EmployeeConn that I'll connect to the database with.

The main script starts by telling EmployeeConn to Open the database (line 11). The parameter value is a String (a text value) that contains ODBC connection string values separated by semicolons. The DSN value identifies the data source, and the UID gives the user id to log in with. If the user must supply a password, you add a PWD value with the password.

Lines 12–16 show how to use the Connection's Execute method to create a Recordset object connected to data in the database. Execute sends a SQL statement to the database, and returns the data rows in a Recordset object that I assign to an object variable (created automatically by VBScript) called rs.

Line 17's if checks the Recordset's Eof property to find out if there are any records before proceeding. If there are, it prints out the header—remember that the HTML inside the if only goes out if the condition is true—then it starts the table.

Do you remember that the IDC had a begindetail...enddetail section that was executed once for each row in the result? ASP doesn't have this, so you have to write the loop yourself. To put out the rows of data in the table, I use the while statement. When the interpreter gets to the while in line 32, rs.Eof is false (I already checked that in the if), so it goes into the loop in lines 33 through 45. The HTML there consists of one row of the table, with special ASP value statements at the appropriate places to put the column values at the right place in each row.

A shortcut to send a column value from a Recordset into the HTML output is <%=rsname("columnName")%>. Use this by itself in HTML in your script (not inside a script block) to place the value of a column at that spot in the HTML, as you see at lines 37, 38, and 41. You can't put any other code in between the script delimiters, but this is very useful for filling in repeated items in your ASP, like HTML SELECT tags or rows in an HTML table, as in the example.

After the HTML for the row, I call rs.MoveNext (line 45) to go to the next row in the Recordset, and then close the while statement with wend. When ASP sees the wend, it goes back up to the while and checks the condition again; if the MoveNext passed the last row in the Recordset, rs.Eof is true and ASP skips to the next line after the wend. The rest of the HTML is sent to the user, and script processing is complete.

Employee.asp is shown in Listing 9.3 and Figure 9.2. You should be able to read through it on your own now because it does essentially the same thing as the index script, with one exception. Just as in Employee.htx, the script needs to retrieve the EmployeeID value to query the database. The WHERE line in the query (line 25) shows how to concatenate the value from the Request object to the end of the query string.

LISTING 9.3   ASP Employee Datasheet: Employee.asp

```
INPUT
 1: <HTML>
 2: <HEAD>
 3: <title>Employee datasheet</title>
 4: </HEAD>
 5: <BODY>
 6: <OBJECT RUNAT=server PROGID=ADODB.Connection
    id=EmployeeConn> </OBJECT>
 7: <P>
 8: <%
 9:     EmployeeConn.Open( "DSN=nwind7;UID=sa" )
10:
11:     ' with ASP, we don't convert() the notes column
12:     set rs = EmployeeConn.Execute( _
13:       "SELECT e.TitleOfCourtesy cTitle, "+_
14:       " e.FirstName + ' ' + e.LastName ename, "+_
15:       " boss.FirstName +' '+ boss.LastName bossName,"+_
16:       " boss.EmployeeID AS bossID, "+_
17:       " e.Title title, " +_
18:       " convert(varchar(10), e.BirthDate, 101) bday, "+_
```

continues

LISTING 9.3   Continued

```
19:         "   convert(varchar(10), e.HireDate, 101) hday, "+_
20:         "   e.Extension extension, "+_
21:         "   e.notes notes " +_
22:         "FROM Employees e "+_
23:         "LEFT OUTER JOIN Employees boss
24:         "             ON boss.EmployeeID = e.ReportsTo "+_
25:         "WHERE  e.EmployeeID = " + Request("EmployeeID") )
26:
27:         if not rs.eof then
28:         %>
29:             <h1>
30:                 Employee information for
31:                 <%=rs("ctitle")%> <%=rs("ename")%>
32:             </h1>
33:             <hr>
34:             Employee ID: <%=Request("EmployeeID")%><br>
35:             Position: <%=rs("title")%><br>
36:             Hired on: <%=rs("hday")%><br>
37:             Phone : x<%=rs("extension")%><br>
38:             Supervisor:
39:                 <A HREF="Employee.asp?EmployeeID=
40:                     <%=rs("bossID")%>">
41:                     <%=rs("bossName")%>
42:                 </A><br>
43:             Notes:<br>
44:             <em><%=rs("notes")%></em><br>
45:             <hr>
46:             <A HREF="EmpIndex.asp">
47:                 Return</A> to the employee index.
48:         <%
49:         else
50:         %>
51:             <h2>An error occurred retrieving the employee.
52:             </h2>
53:         <%
54:         end if
55: %>
56: </BODY>
57: </HTML>
```

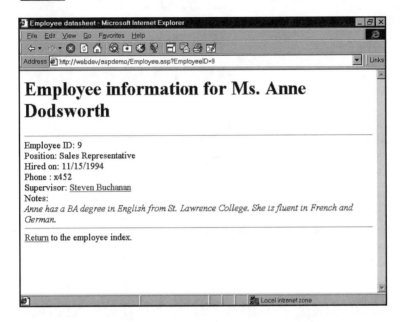

FIGURE 9.2   Employee Data Sheet from ASP.

You should also take note of the continuation (an underscore) at the end of the line after each plus sign in lines 12 through 25. This tells VBScript that the statement continues to the next line; concatenating the strings together to make the SQL this way isn't necessary, but again, it makes it easier for you to read and see what it's doing. It's important to keep code easy to read—it makes it harder to write bugs!

Summary

This chapter has introduced you to the primary Microsoft technology for high-powered Web sites: Active Server Pages. I've shown you the basics of VBScript and how to use VBScript variables, objects, and statements with ActiveX Data Objects to retrieve data in the same manner you did with IDC. In the next lesson, you're going to see some more features of ASP as you go through design and implementation of a Web application based on IIS and SQL Server 7.

LESSON 10

An Interactive Web Application

This lesson will demonstrate designing and implementing a Web application, including designing the database, selecting the publishing technology, and building the application.

In this lesson, I'll walk through designing and building an interactive application based on SQL Server and ASP. Specifying, designing, and building applications is a major field of study. The approach you'll learn here is a fast and efficient method for building small applications like the ones you'll probably build for your intranet.

Deciding What to Do: Step by Step

Before you do anything related to building tables or Web pages, you have to decide what it is you're going to do. I know, it sounds like a no-brainer, but many applications are started by building user interfaces and tables, and then completed by redoing half of them because the need wasn't fully understood!

Listing What Is Needed

When you're deciding what to do in your project, write down ahead of time what data you or your users will need, and what functions they will need to perform. It's very important that you not say how the computer is going to do something; instead, describe what you need the computer to provide. That leaves you free to select the best way of doing it later.

In this lesson, you're going to build a guest book for your Web site. The guest book should satisfy these needs:

- The application should let visitors see who has signed the guest book.

- The application should let a visitor sign the guest book.

- When visitors sign the guest book, they should be able to record the following: name, email address, favorite activity, and a note (comments).

- Later, the application might need to provide additional features based on who the user is.

The first two requirements are functional: They state what the site should let a user do. The third is a data requirement, in that it tells what information should be stored. The last requirement is one that you will get, though you won't want to. It says, in effect, I don't know what I'll want to do, but your site should be able to accommodate it. *C'est la vie.*

The first requirement could have said: The application should have a page that shows visitors who have signed the guest book. Describing it that way dictates that you have to have a page in your solution specifically to show previous visitors, but that might not be what you want. Again, describe what you need, not how to do it.

Designing the Interface

The user interface for your application is the Web pages that you're going to create. It will help lay out what you're going to do if you create a site diagram now. If you're building the site for yourself, you will be able to tell what needs to be done next at any point in time. If you're doing it for someone else, it also will help eliminate any misunderstandings. In Figure 10.1, I have decided to use three pages: one for the main guest book page, one to show comments, and one to add an entry. The fourth script saves the data from the form and jumps back to the main page.

You can also sketch in graphics, layout, or other design elements that you want to see in the finished product.

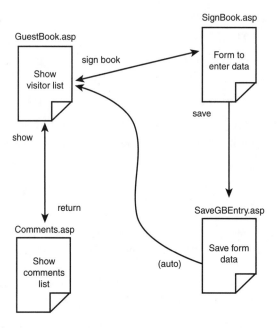

FIGURE 10.1 Guestbook site diagram.

Describing the Data

After you've decided on the requirements, you need to describe what data you need to store. It helps to draw out the items in a diagram like Figure 10.2. This *logical data model* should show the data needed, not how to record it in the database. You might want to include estimated data sizes (like how many characters can go in a name). You should base this on the data needs in the requirements and on whatever additional data your user interface design needs. Check and recheck your work to make sure you include as much as you can of the data you'll have to store; it can be very difficult to change this after you've built your application.

In this diagram, I've drawn a box for each entity in the problem, with lines between related objects. Where one item is associated with several other items, the crow's feet indicates the "several" end.

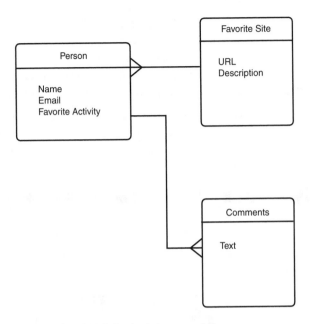

FIGURE 10.2   Guestbook logical data model.

Finally, you should describe the *physical data model*, the description of how you'll store the data in the database. Figure 10.3 shows the physical model I'll use for the guestbook. There are many tools for drawing these diagrams; I used the diagrammer in Microsoft Visual InterDev, but you'll want a dedicated design tool if you do this often.

The physical data model states what tables and relations you will use to store the entities from the logical data model. In general, you should follow a procedure similar to this:

1. Start with your logical data model. The entities are your candidate tables, and their attributes are columns in the tables.

2. Look at each attribute: If the values that will go in it should be drawn from a small number of predefined values, separate them out into a lookup table. The table they come from will need a foreign key to refer to the lookup table, so add that. In the example, you're going to provide predefined types of favorite activities, so move it out to its own table.

3. Pick a primary key for each table. This should be the smallest
piece of data that uniquely identifies a row in the table (in the
Person table, for example, I chose the name). If nothing presents
itself directly, and sometimes it won't, you can use an identity
value, a numeric id you assign. Try to avoid these if you can.

Some tables won't need a primary key, but these are rare. Only
tables that completely depend on others (they do not store entities
themselves) can omit a primary key. In the example, the Comment
table is one of these.

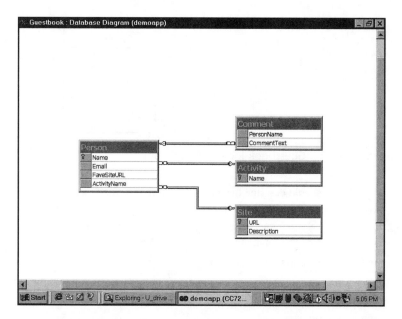

Figure 10.3   Guestbook physical data model.

   Note   There's animated debate even now regarding
selection of primary keys. Some people prefer the
approach I've described, others prefer using identity
values whenever they can. Pick the dogma that barks
best for you.

4. Look for attributes that really aren't part of the entity you're storing. This can be a subjective decision; in the example, I've decided that the *comment* isn't part of the person, but the name and email are. The favorite Web site might be or not. I separated it, just in case.

5. If you're going to store large data items like text or image fields, it's generally a good idea to put these in a separate table.

Refer back to Lesson 2, "Understanding Databases," for a refresher on the kinds of information you can put in your database. When you've completed this step, you have described all the tables and relations you will have in your database.

Double Checking

So you're done, right? Well... maybe. Now is the time to take a sanity check. Step back and look at what you've described and ask yourself the following questions:

1. *Does it meet the requirement?* If you're doing it for someone else, show it to them and ask the same thing.

2. *Do you know what it is you're going to build?* Try to get that straight before you move on; you don't have to nail every detail, but the better your understanding now, the better your site will be in the end.

After you have completed these steps, you'll have a solid start in building your application. If you're building it with other people, everyone will know what it is you're going to build. Even if you're only building it for yourself, you'll be much better off because you have a roadmap of what to do. My experience has been that, even for a seemingly small application like this, planning pays.

Selecting a Publishing Method

The three Web publishing methods I've discussed, in order of increasing complexity, are the Web Assistant Wizard, IDC, and ASP. You can use Table 10.1 to help pick a technology.

TABLE 10.1 Choosing a Publishing Technology

If you need...	Then you can use...
Read-only, static pages from data	Web Assistant Wizard
Simple forms or queries; just work with the database	Internet Data Connector
Anything more	Active Server Pages

IDC is a good tool if you want to work only with the database, or if much of your application's code will be in stored procedures there. ASP is a better choice when you might want to expand the application later, if you need to work with services in addition to SQL Server, or if you want to have more features in the scripts you write for your application than you can implement with IDC.

I'm going to use ASP for this application because of the last requirement. Because I don't know what the additional features might be, I need to keep my options open.

Now that you have a description of what to build, there are a couple of things about VBScript that you need to look at, and then you'll see how to translate this design into an ASP application.

Handling Updates

You have two options when updating data from an ASP script: either directly updating with SQL, or using a Recordset. Neither one is intrinsically easier, necessarily, but I often use SQL because it doesn't require creating a Recordset and the additional network traffic and processing that involves.

To use a direct SQL update, all you need to do is tell the Connection to Execute a SQL statement as you did in the last lesson. There, the statement was a retrieval, but it can just as easily be an UPDATE or INSERT, as in the following:

```
Conn.Execute("INSERT MyTable( field1, field2 )
VALUES( val1, val2 )")
```

This statement inserts a row into the mythical MyTable table. If all your inserts were like this, this would definitely be the way to go, but you'll usually construct your SQL from Request properties (the values the user sent you), so you might choose to use a Recordset, instead.

To use a Recordset, you first create a Recordset variable on the table you're updating. If you're adding a row, you call the Recordset's AddNew method. Then, set its row properties to the values you want in the row, and call its Update method. Listing 10.1 shows creating a row in the Shippers table in Northwind.

LISTING 10.1   Adding a Shipper to the Database

```
set rs = Server.CreateObject( "ADODB.Recordset" )
    rs.Open "Shippers", EmployeeConn, _
            adOpenStatic, adLockPessimistic
        rs.AddNew
            rs("CompanyName") = Request("CompanyName")
            rs("Phone") = Request("Phone")
        rs.Update
    rs.Close
set rs = Nothing
```

The cursor type and locking constants, the third and fourth parameters to Recordset.Open, are defined in adovbs.inc on IIS4. You can use the values I do or see the ADO documentation for available settings.

In this example, the script is invoked as the action of an HTML form containing fields named CompanyName and Phone. It creates a new row in the Shippers table with the data the user filled in.

To update a row, you create the Recordset using a SELECT that retrieves the row to update, assign values to its fields, and then call Update to apply the changes.

Guest Book Example

There isn't much more to say about the site, so here's the code. You might think it odd to write the code before building databases and all that, but it's not. Because I've done the database design already, you know what the tables and columns are, and you can write the pages even though the database isn't built yet. If you're working with other people on the project, you

can divide up the work without having to finish the database before the
scripts.

I've reformatted the HTML in Listings 10.2–10.5 to a degree; the HTML
is typical, though, of what you'll see when using a development tool to
create your sites. It is a challenge to preserve a format across all the
scripts in the site.

LISTING 10.2   Guestbook.asp

`INPUT`

```
 1: <% Option Explicit %>
 2: <% Response.Expires = 0 %>
 3: <HTML>
 4: <HEAD>
 5: <%
 6:     Dim GBConn, RSPerson
 7:
 8:     ' Creating objects in script instead of the OBJECT tag
 9:     Set GBConn = Server.CreateObject("ADODB.Connection")
10:     Set RSPerson = _
11:             Server.CreateObject( "ADODB.Recordset" )
12:
13:     GBConn.Open( "DSN=Guestbook;UID=sa" )      ' Connect
14:     RSPerson.Open "Person", GBConn
15: %>
16: </HEAD>
17: <BODY>
18: <font face=Helvetica>
19: <P>Thanks for coming by! Below are some of my recent
20: visitors. I hope you'll <A href="SignBook.asp">leave your
21: name</A>, too.</P>
22: <P>
23: <TABLE align=center border=0
24:         cellPadding=1 cellSpacing=1 width=75% >
25:     <TR bgColor=gray >
26:         <TD align=middle><font Color=white>Name</font>
27:             </TD>
28:         <TD align=middle><font Color=white>Email</font>
29:             </TD>
30:         <TD align=middle><font Color=white>
31:             Favorite Activity</font></TD></TR>
32:     <% while not RSPerson.EOF %>
33:     <TR>
34:         <TD><%=RSPerson("Name")%></TD>
```

```
35:          <TD><%=RSPerson("Email")%></TD>
36:          <TD><%=RSPerson("ActivityName")%></TD>
37:      </TR>
38:      <%      RSPerson.MoveNext
39:          wend %>
40: </TABLE></P>
41: <P>You can also take a look at the <A
42: href="comments.asp">comments</A> I'm getting.</P>
43: </font>
44: </BODY>
45: </HTML>
```

ANALYSIS GuestBook.asp displays the names and emails of visitors who
have signed the guest book, by creating the RSPerson Recordset on the
Person table (line 14), then creating an HTML table with the data from
the database table (lines 23 to 40). It includes two links, one to the
SignBook.asp page (on line 20) to leave an entry, and one to
Comments.asp (on line 42) to see what comments people have made.

LISTING 10.3   SignBook.asp

```
 1: <% Option Explicit %>
 2: <HTML>
 3: <HEAD>
 4: <%  ' Use the Activity table to populate the activity
 5:      ' SELECT control.
 6:      Dim GBConn
 7:      Dim RSActivity
 8:
 9:      Set GBConn = Server.CreateObject("ADODB.Connection")
10:      Set RSActivity = _
11:              Server.CreateObject( "ADODB.Recordset" )
12:
13:      GBConn.Open( "DSN=Guestbook;UID=sa" )
14:      RSActivity.Open "Activity", GBConn
15: %>
16: </HEAD>
17: <BODY>
18: <font face=Helvetica>
19: <% ' Form to accept data for the guestbook %>
20: <hr>
21: <h4>Please enter the information below
22:      and click &quot;save.&quot;</h4>
23: <hr>
```

continues

LISTING 10.3   Continued

```
24: <FORM action="SaveGBEntry.asp" id=GuestForm
25:         method=post name=GuestForm>
26: <p><input type="submit" value="Save"></p>
27: <TABLE WIDTH=75% BORDER=0 CELLSPACING=1 CELLPADDING=1>
28:     <TR>
29:         <TD align=right>Your name:</TD>
30:         <TD><input name="Name" maxLength=100 size=50>
31:         </TD>
32:     </TR>
33:     <TR>
34:         <TD align=right>Your email:</TD>
35:         <TD><input name="Email" maxLength=100 size=50>
36:         </TD>
37:     </TR>
38:     <TR>
39:         <TD align=right>URL of your favorite web site:
40:         </TD>
41:         <TD><input name="FaveSiteURL" maxLength=100
42:             size=50></TD>
43:     </TR>
44:     <TR>
45:         <TD align=right>Type of activity you prefer:
46:         </TD>
47:         <TD><SELECT name="ActivityName">
48:             <% while not RSActivity.EOF %>
49:                 <OPTION value="<%=RSActivity("Name")%>">
50:                     <%=RSActivity("Name")%>
51:             <% RSActivity.MoveNext
52:                 wend
53:                 %>
54:             </SELECT>
55:         </TD>
56:     </TR>
57:     <TR>
58:         <TD align=center colspan=2>
59:             Your judicious pronouncements:<br>
60:             <textarea name="Comments" rows=20 cols=50>
61:                 empty
62:             </textarea>
63:         </TD>
64:     </TR>
65: </TABLE>
66:
67: </FORM>
68: </font>
69: </BODY></HTML>
```

ANALYSIS   SignBook.asp and SaveGBEntry.asp show one way to enter data into the database. I use one page with the form and another with the code that updates the database with data the user entered. When you want users to input data, you'll usually take this approach; Microsoft examples demonstrate using the same file for the form and update code, but I personally think it's too confusing.

SignBook.asp has a single form in it starting at line 24 and ending at line 67, with a POST method that invokes SaveGBEntry.asp. Each form field (INPUT, SELECT, and TEXTAREA tags) is named so that SaveGBEntry.asp can retrieve the data easily. When the user clicks the Save submit button, the data in the form are sent to the server, where SaveGBEntry.asp is loaded to process it.

SignBook.asp also shows how to use lookup tables in your forms. Since the activity is a lookup in the database (the user can't add new activities) it should be presented to the user as a drop-down listbox on the form, using the SELECT HTML tag. The code in lines 47–54 uses the RSActivity Recordset to scan the Activity table and create a SELECT with choices for each activity. If you later add new activity choices to the database table, your form will automatically make those choices available to users. If you later delete activities from the database that no one uses, they will no longer show up on the form.

LISTING **10.4**   SaveGBEntry.asp

INPUT

```
 1: <%Option Explicit%>
 2: <HTML>
 3: <HEAD>
 4: </HEAD>
 5: <BODY>
 6: <% ' Save data from SignBook.asp to the database %>
 7: <font face=Helvetica>
 8: <P><em>Saving entry...</em></P>
 9: </font>
10: <%' the above text is on the screen until the data
11:    ' is saved, then JScript at the end jumps back to the
12:    ' table index.
13:       Dim GBConn
14:       Dim RSURL, RSPerson, RSComment
15:
16:       ' get on the database
```

continues

LISTING 10.4   Continued

```
17:        Set GBConn = Server.CreateObject("ADODB.Connection")
18:        GBConn.Open( "DSN=Guestbook;UID=sa" )
19:
20:        ' make the updates; have to update in the order
21:        ' shown due to table dependencies.
22:
23:        ' query Site and add URL only if it doesn't exist
24:        Set RSURL = GBConn.Execute( "SELECT * FROM Site " + _
25:            "WHERE URL='" + Request("FaveSiteURL") + "'" )
26:        if RSURL.Eof then
27:            GBConn.Execute "INSERT Site(URL,Description)" + _
28:                " VALUES( '" + Request("FaveSiteURL") + _
29:                        "', 'Auto added' )"
30:        end if
31:
32:        ' Person: insert new or update existing
33:        Set RSPerson = GBConn.Execute( _
34:            "SELECT * FROM Person " + _
35:            "WHERE Name = '" + Request("Name") + "'" )
36:        if ( RSPerson.Eof ) then
37:            GBConn.Execute _
38:                "INSERT Person( Name, Email, " + _
39:                              "FaveSiteURL,ActivityName) "+ _
40:                "VALUES( '" + Request("Name") + "', " + _
41:                    "'" + Request("Email") + "', " + _
42:                    "'" + Request("FaveSiteURL") + "', " + _
43:                    "'" + Request("ActivityName") + "' )"
44:        else
45:            GBConn.Execute "UPDATE Person "+ _
46:                "SET Email='" + Request("Email") + "', " + _
47:                "FaveSiteURL='"+Request("FaveSiteURL") + _
48:                "', " + _
49:                "ActivityName='"+Request("ActivityName") + _
50:                "' " + _
51:                "WHERE Name='" + Request("Name") + "'"
52:        end if
53:
54:        ' no PK on the Comments table
55:        Set RSComment = _
56:            Server.CreateObject( "ADODB.Recordset" )
57:        RSComment.Open "dbo.Comment", GBConn,
58:            adOpenStatic, adLockPessimistic
59:        RSComment.AddNew
60:            RSComment("PersonName") = Request("Name")
61:            RSComment("CommentText") = Request("Comments")
62:        RSComment.Update
63:
```

```
64:      ' lastly, jump the user back to the main page with
65:      ' client side script: %>
66: <SCRIPT Language="JavaScript">
67:      location = "GuestBook.asp"
68: </SCRIPT>
69:
70: </BODY></HTML>
```

ANALYSIS SaveGBEntry.asp demonstrates updating multiple tables (Site, Person, and Comment) from the data on a form. As I noted in line 20, the code has to update the database in the order shown. When it inserts a record into the Person table, which has a foreign key reference to Site, it must have already created the row in Site that the Person row references. If not, the INSERT into Person will fail.

Because I don't want to have the same site multiple times in Site, the code in lines 24 and 25 checks the database to see if the site is already in the database. If it isn't, it's recorded in lines 27–29, but otherwise not.

People have more data than sites, however. Lines 33–35 check the Person table to see if the person already exists; if the person isn't found, it creates a new record in lines 37–43. Instead of just moving on if the person is found, though, the else clause in lines 44–52 will update the Person record with the information on the form if the user already exists in the database. Though you might not want to use this code for an Internet site (imagine John Smith in California replacing data for John Smith in Nova Scotia!), I present the technique to demonstrate optionally creating or updating rows with ASP.

Another technique demonstrated by the script gives the user feedback as it is working. Over slow links or on heavily loaded servers, a significant amount of time can elapse while your code updates the database. Right after the opening of the BODY section of the page, therefore, a text message goes to the user saying the server is saving the data (see line 8). Because the server goes from the beginning to the end of the script line by line, and there's no more HTML sent to the user until line 65, this message will be on the user's screen until the database updates are complete. When the server finishes executing the database code, lines 65 through 70 are sent to the browser; the JavaScript in line 66 redirects (jumps) the browser back to the main GuestBook.asp page.

You're creating a user interface when you build a Web site, and little things like immediate feedback mean a lot to users, who will otherwisebe clicking buttons over and over and wondering why your server isn't responding. In larger, more complicated operations, you can place additional messages in the script to tell the user as the operations progress. Generally, the more information you give users on what's going on, the happier they'll be with your application.

LISTING 10.5   Comments.asp

INPUT

```
 1: <%Option Explicit%>
 2: <%Response.Expires = 0%>
 3: <HTML>
 4: <HEAD>
 5: <title>Comment Page</title>
 6: </HEAD>
 7: <BODY>
 8: <font face=Helvetica>
 9: <P>Comments on my site:</P>
10: <TABLE border=1 cellPadding=3 cellSpacing=1 width=75%>
11: <%    Dim GBConn, RSComment
12:
13:      ' get on the database
14:      Set GBConn = Server.CreateObject("ADODB.Connection")
15:      GBConn.Open( "DSN=Guestbook;UID=sa" )
16:
17:      Set RSComment = _
18:          GBConn.Execute( "SELECT * FROM Comment" )
19:      while not RSComment.Eof
20: %>   <TR>
21:          <TD align=right vAlign=top>
22:              <%=RSComment("PersonName")%> said:
23:          </TD>
24:          <TD><%=RSComment("CommentText")%></TD>
25:      </TR>
26: <%
27:      RSComment.MoveNext
28:      wend
29: %>
30: </TABLE>
31: </font>
32: </BODY></HTML>
```

Comments.asp is a simple page to show the users what comments are in the database, along with the name of the user that made the comment.

Figure 10.4 shows the start page, GuestBook.asp.

FIGURE 10.4 Guest book start page.

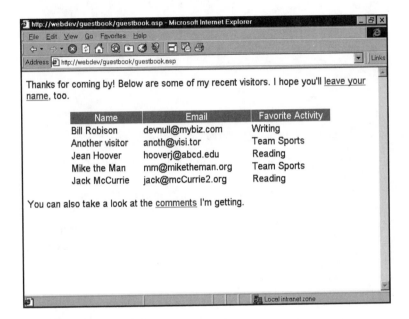

Summary

This should have been an interesting lesson for you. I discussed the importance of planning your Web application, and stepped through a specific method to define your requirements, design your solution, and then implement it with IIS and SQL Server. The lesson's example, the most complicated one in the book, demonstrated implementing a design using ASP and ADO.

Now that you've seen the application side, I'm going to go back to SQL Server and take a look at performance and retrieval topics you should be aware of, and then I'll look at how to implement the database tables your guest book application uses.

LESSON 11

Improving Query Performance

In this lesson, you'll learn how to use SQL Server's Query Analyzer to explore and improve how SQL Server satisfies your queries.

So, let's say your database is up and working, and you and three other people are using it. It does everything you need it to, except the coffee thing, and life is good. Then colleagues in another department discover your application might help their work, too, so they start using it for their data. Quite flattering, but then more users start working the system and it starts to get *slooowww*. Users start anthropomorphizing the hourglass cursor. Other databases on the server are affected, and the DBA wants to know what *you* are going to do about it.

At this point, you can't do anything. You don't even know what's wrong! Take note of a concept I borrowed from another profession: First, do no harm. You can as easily slow things down with an imperfect understanding as speed them up, so until you have measured performance and know what the problem is, don't try to fix it.

This lesson will show you how the server executes your queries and how to use Query Analyzer to explore query execution, identify problems, and evaluate the effects of changes you make to address those problems. For large queries, I will use the Internet server log for one of my servers, in the table `inetlog`, because the sample databases do not contain enough data. The table is the standard format used for IIS logging, but I have added an integer ID field to demonstrate some indexing techniques. For other examples, I'll use the `pubs` database.

Tuning query performance is a large part, but still only a part, of managing your server's performance. Any server resource that is heavily used, such as the disks or memory, will limit the performance of all applications that need to use it. When several applications require the same resource at the same time, a situation called *resource contention* occurs, and each must wait its turn before it can proceed. If the condition persists, that resource becomes a bottleneck that governs the performance of the entire server. Discerning and repairing this sort of server-wide problem is the task of the system administrator or the DBA, but this lesson will help you help them, by reducing your own demands on the server.

Execution Plans

When you send a query, SQL Server follows three main steps to satisfy it:

1. The query is *parsed*, a process in which SQL Server reads the query text and breaks it down to understand what you are asking it to do.

2. SQL Server's optimizer reads information about the structure, indexing, and amount of data in the tables that you are querying. It uses this information to form a *query plan*, the steps it will follow to achieve the results you requested.

3. In the last step, SQL Server carries out the steps in the query plan to satisfy your request.

By planning the query in advance, SQL Server can select the most efficient method to accomplish the desired results.

To select the best query plan, SQL Server's optimizer attempts to minimize the server resources used in satisfying the request. The most important of these resources is usually the I/O cost, but CPU performance can become a problem in some cases as well. You can inspect the costs incurred by your query with the SHOWPLAN_ALL option in queries or with Query Analyzer's graphical display—a much more approachable method.

The textual execution plan is turned on by executing the SET SHOWPLAN_ALL ON statement before the query you want to optimize, or by using the Connection Options dialog in Query Analyzer, as in Figure 11.1. You get to this dialog by selecting Current Connection Options from the Query menu.

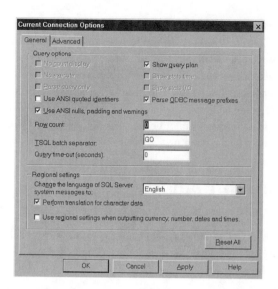

FIGURE 11.1   Execution plan turned on in Query Analyzer.

Looking for the client hosts in the Internet log produces the following results:

INPUT

```
select clienthost
from inetlog
```

OUTPUT

```
StmtText
----------------------------------------
select clienthost
from inetlog

(1 row(s) affected)

StmtText
----------------------------------------------------------------
  |--Table Scan(OBJECT:([demoapp].[dbo].[inetlog]))

(1 row(s) affected)
```

In the output, SQL Server echoes the SQL you told it to execute back to you, and then tells you what it is going to do. In this case, it says it will execute only one step in the query: scan the table and retrieve all rows from the `inetlog` table. Because this table has more than 200,000 rows in it, this will be a pretty lengthy operation. You can see the cost of a query by going back to the connection options, turning off the execution plan, and turning on Show stats I/O. The results resemble the following when you execute the same query:

OUTPUT

```
SQL Server Execution Times:
    CPU time = 0 ms,  elapsed time = 0 ms.
SQL Server parse and compile time:
    CPU time = 0 ms, elapsed time = 165 ms.
SQL Server parse and compile time:
    CPU time = 0 ms, elapsed time = 0 ms.
clienthost
- - - - - - - - - - - - - - - - - - - - - - - - - - - - - - - - - - - - - - - - - - - - - - - - - -

(result rows omitted)

(207280 row(s) affected)

Table 'inetlog'. Scan count 1, logical reads 4118, physical
reads 1674, read-ahead reads 4120.

SQL Server Execution Times:
    CPU time = 0 ms,  elapsed time = 297672 ms.
SQL Server parse and compile time:
    CPU time = 0 ms, elapsed time = 5 ms.

SQL Server Execution Times:
    CPU time = 0 ms,  elapsed time = 0 ms.
```

Notice how long this query took, even though the query was run locally on the server? Back in Lesson 2, "Understanding Databases," I mentioned that you would rarely use unconstrained queries, ones with no WHERE clause to reduce the number of rows returned. This is why. Such a *long running query*, a term you'll see in the Books Online, can tie up a server and affect other users.

Very little of the almost five minutes the query required to execute was used in processing the data; the query only asked it to read all the rows and return the clienthost column, so there wasn't really any processing required. The real time-waster was I/O.

SQL Server tries to minimize the number of times it has to read data from the disk by keeping a copy of each piece of data it reads in an area of memory called a *cache*. Old or infrequently used data is gradually replaced in the cache with newer information, but while an item is there, SQL Sever can retrieve it from the cache instead of going out to the disk.

You can see how much SQL Server is using the disk, and something of how well the cache is being used, in the first line of the last block of statistics, which includes the following:

- *Logical reads*: How many times SQL Server needed data from the disk

- *Physical reads*: How many times the needed data had to be read from disk because it wasn't in the cache memory

- *Read-ahead reads*: How many times SQL Server read more data into the cache than was requested, in anticipation of needing it later

In the example, SQL Server did a good job of reading data, since it required data 4,118 times (logical reads) but only issued 1,674 physical reads. The query still took a long time, though, just because of the amount of data it had to get from the disk.

The textual execution plan is useful if you have to use a tool other than Query Analyzer (for example, if you also have SQL Server 6.5 clients), but Query Analyzer provides a much more accessible interface in its graphical execution plan display. Selecting Show Execution Plan on the Query menu turns on this feature. This is not the same thing as turning on the Show query plan option in the Connection options dialog box; in fact, you can't use this tool at the same time as those plan and statistics options.

When you run a query with the graphical execution plan turned on, you'll have another tab under the results pane called Execution Plan. Selecting this tab after the query completes will show you a graphical rendering of the query's execution.

To display the query plan in Figure 11.2, execute the following query in the pubs database with the graphical execution plan on:

```
SELECT au_lname, title
FROM authors
JOIN titleauthor ON authors.au_id = titleauthor.au_id
JOIN titles ON titles.title_id = titleauthor.title_id
```

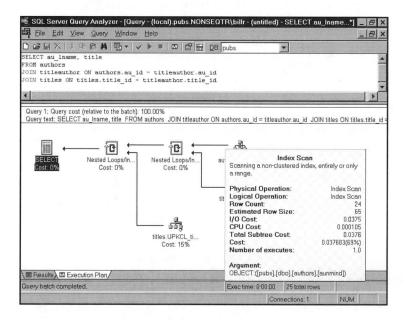

FIGURE 11.2   Graphical Execution plan in Query Analyzer.

The graphic display shows the same steps you would see in the textual execution plan: Each icon in the display shows a step in the process, and each arrow indicates data passed from one step to another. The icon at the far left is the root statement you executed, and the operations to the right are the steps into which SQL Server broke the operations. If you move your mouse over a processing step, a window appears with the information described in Table 11.1.

TABLE 11.1 Information on a Processing Step

Item	Description
Description	In general, what the step is
Physical Operation	What the step does
Logical Operation	The SQL operation it performs
Row Count	Number of rows produced by this process
Estimated Row Size	Approximate average row size produced
I/O Cost	Time used for disk operations
CPU Cost	Time CPU was processing information
Total Subtree Cost	Time in this step and all to the right
Cost	Time in this step
Number of executes	Number of times the step is repeated
Argument	The command the step will perform

If you move your cursor over one of the arrows, you see the size and number of rows that were passed from the lower level operation to the higher one (that is, from the right to the left). Multiplying the size by the number of rows, you can estimate the amount of data passed from the lower to the higher processing step.

This is a wonderfully useful and easy-to-use tool for displaying query performance. I hope you'll take a few minutes to explore it. You can gain a lot of insight into the way the database works just by executing different queries and looking at what SQL Server has to do to satisfy them. Now take a look at how you can use indices to change the performance of your queries.

Index Analysis

As you might imagine, there is more to performance than how long the query takes to execute. In my table-scanning query from `inetlog`, most of the time executing was involved in reading data from the disk; the CPU time was negligible. In client/server applications, there are generally three areas in which you can improve performance:

- Client/server communication
- Server CPU time
- Server disk time

Improving client-server communication, governed by the network traffic between the database server and the client, requires mainly that you retrieve only the data you need from the database, only as often as you must. Server CPU time is usually not a large factor in database performance, although it can be if you are correlating a large amount of data or doing a lot of calculations.

The simple fact is that your bottleneck is usually going to be the disks. The most accessible way to improve individual statement execution times is usually with an index (or several). As I've discussed, an index is a structure that SQL Server can read to select the rows it will use from a table instead of reading the table itself. Because the index is usually much smaller than the table, the server can sometimes keep the index cached in memory. In the worst case, it might have to read the index in from disk, but it's reading far less data than it would be if it had to read the whole table.

The operations that should receive attention are those that are requiring a large amount of resources and a large percentage of the query's cost. If the process's main resource use is CPU time, you can try precalculating data putting it in a separate table that you refresh at intervals. More commonly, you'll find a process with a large I/O cost; for these, you can try either better constraining the query to reduce the amount of data retrieved in that step, or using an index to speed up that process.

 Note The SQL Server documentation advises using a clustered index for fields that you will use in range or specific matches, as you would for a primary key. I have seen mixed results in following this advice, so my advice remains: Measure the effect of indices on performance to find the best solution. Don't depend on a formula; depend on results.

The syntax for creating an index is as follows:

SYNTAX

```
CREATE [UNIQUE] [CLUSTERED ¦ NONCLUSTERED] INDEX indexname
ON tableref( columnref [, columnref ...]
[ WITH options ]
```

A UNIQUE index prohibits inserting duplicate data in the column(s) it indexes. Creating a UNIQUE index on a column does not create a UNIQUE constraint on the column, but adding a UNIQUE constraint creates a corresponding index.

A CLUSTERED index, of which only one can be created on a table, orders the rows as they are physically stored in the database file. NONCLUSTERED indices are stored outside the table and do not affect the table's storage arrangement; there can be up to 249 of these per table.

Note   There are several options you can use when creating an index to modify how it is stored and used by SQL Server. This subject is beyond the scope of this lesson because it requires more knowledge of the physical storage of the database than I can show you. The options are not commonly used, however, so I'm comfortable with skipping them.

The following example creates a nonclustered index named idx_ClientHost on the ClientHost column of the inetlog table:

```
CREATE INDEX idx_ClientHost
ON inetlog( ClientHost )
```

In general, you should create an index when a processing step in the query plan is indicating a table scan produces a large number of disk reads. For example, in the inetlog table, counting the unique values of the ClientHost column took 5.81 seconds on my computer without an index, of which 4.5 seconds was used scanning the table on the disk. Creating the index as shown previously reduced the total time to 1.38 seconds because it replaced the table scan with an index scan requiring only 0.8 seconds, and cut in half the amount of data used by higher processes.

Once again, whatever you do, measure the results. My favorite tactic for quick results is to use three windows in Query Analyzer with the following steps:

1. Turn on the execution plan display in window 1, and execute the query you need to improve.

2. In the second window, create the index.

3. When creation finishes, go to the third window, turn on the execution plan display, and execute the same query as in step 1.

You now have one window showing the execution plan and statistics without the index, and one showing performance with it. You can move back and forth between the two displays to compare the results.

Why not index everything? Well, there are issues:

- Indices take up disk space, of course, so creating them all over the place without measured performance gains is a waste.

- The optimizer might not gain anything from an index; if a column in the database only has two possible values, your return on disk investment will not be nearly as dramatic. Because the index is supposed to reduce the number or size of the rows that have to be processed by the server, an index on a row with this sort of data could *reduce* performance by increasing the amount of I/O the server must perform.

- An index slows update, insert and delete operations, because SQL Server has to modify the index in addition to the table. Remember: measure performance before and after you make a change, and only keep a change that creates significant improvement. If an index doesn't help, *drop it.*

Summary

The information in this lesson is less important to you if you are working with small databases with a limited number of users. As your clientele grows, however, performance will rapidly become an issue, and you need to understand how to find the bottlenecks in your server.

In this lesson, you learned how SQL Server plans and executes your queries, and how to use Query Analyzer to show textual and graphical descriptions of both the execution plan and resources used during query execution. To address query performance problems

In this lesson, you learned how SQL Server plans and executes your queries, and how to use Query Analyzer to show textual and graphical descriptions of both the execution plan and resouces used during query execution. To address query performance problems, you learned how to create indices, and some tips on their use to increase performance.

LESSON 12

Analyzing Your Data with SQL

In this lesson, you'll learn advanced features of the SELECT statement that you can use to analyze your data and create reports directly from the database.

As you've learned, SQL is a powerful language for data manipulation. You know how to use SQL to

- Rapidly assemble related data from tables storing information on different entities

- Create new data sets from queries

- Update one set of data based on the information derived from others

In this lesson, you're going to explore two additional capabilities of SQL. First, although there are plenty of options in reporting tools available, SQL itself provides simple but capable summarization and reporting capabilities. By performing as much of the analysis functions on the server as possible, subject to limitations in its resources, you can greatly reduce the amount of network capacity and resources needed for your client workstation.

Second, although all the queries you've looked at so far executed in a single level, it is possible to build queries that themselves contain other queries, so that multiple steps to data analysis can be combined, automated, and executed by the server.

Rollups and Summaries

When you've queried the database in the past, you've gotten all of the rows that matched a set of criteria, but quite often you will want a little more—for example, you might want the totals for a series of numerical columns. You could SELECT the rows and then add them up, but SQL gives you a series of operations to *aggregate* rows and perform calculations.

Aggregate   This term can be either a verb, noun, or adjective in this context: When you *aggregate* a group of data items, you are combining them into one piece of data using some rule, and the *aggregate* is the result. Finally, the *aggregate* functions are those that SQL Server provides you to combine (aggregate) data. Simple, huh?

You've already seen one example of an aggregate function: The COUNT function I used to count the number of rows in a result took in the rows from the SELECT, counted them, and then produced the number of rows as the aggregate value. The aggregate functions provided by SQL Server are shown in Table 12.1.

TABLE 12.1   Aggregate Functions in SQL Server

Function	Description
AVG	Computes average of values
COUNT	Counts number of values or rows
DISTINCT	Eliminates duplicate values or rows
MAX	Computes maximum of values
MIN	Computes minimum of values
STDEV, STDEVP	Computes standard deviation, population standard deviation
SUM	Computes sum of values
VAR, VARP	Computes variance, population variance

These functions can be used in any function where a set of rows is expected, for example:

```
SELECT SUM( price * ytd_sales ) FROM titles
```

This query would produce a single figure sum showing all sales recorded in the titles table; generally this wouldn't be a very useful number. So let's try instead to retrieve the names of authors and how much they have sold:

INPUT

```
SELECT au_fname + ' ' + au_lname Name, price*ytd_sales Sales
FROM authors
JOIN titleauthor ON authors.au_id = titleauthor.au_id
JOIN titles ON titleauthor.title_id = titles.title_id
```

OUTPUT

```
Name                                              Sales
------------------------------------------------- --------------
Abraham Bennet                                    81859.0500
Reginald Blotchet-Halls                           180397.2000
Cheryl Carson                                     201501.0000
Michel DeFrance                                   66515.5400
Innes del Castillo                                40619.6800
Ann Dull                                          81900.0000
Marjorie Green                                    81859.0500
Marjorie Green                                    55978.7800
Burt Gringlesby                                   61384.0500
Sheryl Hunter                                     81900.0000
Livia Karsen                                      8096.2500
etc.
```

Oops, that's not right! Marjorie's getting double billing! This statement is going to retrieve each book for each author, and print out the sales *for each individual book*; it's too dumb to figure out that Marjorie Green wrote two of them.

Enter SQL. I promised you a more comprehensive syntax for the statement, so here it is.

```
SELECT { * ¦ columnref [, columnref ... ] }
[INTO newtablename ]
FROM tableref [, tableref ...]
[[INNER ¦ {LEFT ¦ RIGHT} OUTER ] JOIN tableref
    ON columnref = columnref ...]
```

```
[WHERE expression [{AND ¦ OR} expression ...]]
[GROUP BY { ALL ¦ columnref [, columnref ...] } ]
[HAVING expression ]
[ORDER BY columnref, [, columnref ...] [DESC]]
[COMPUTE agg_func [, agg_func ... ]
    [BY orderref [, orderref ...]] ]
```

This still does not show the entirety of the statement, but it's as much as you'll probably ever need. Much of this you've seen or could figure out, but I'll fill in the rest now. The first new item, INTO, is the simplest: SELECT...INTO creates a new table. The results of the query will be stored into a table named *newtablename*.

GROUP BY is the focus of the introductory example. You use this clause to perform a *rollup*, or row summary of your data, using one or more aggregate functions to summarize the grouped columns. In the example, Marjorie's books were generating multiple rows with the sums for each individual book; what I would like to do is group the rows for her together into one row, and sum the sales for each book into one total. Have I given the solution away?

INPUT

```
SELECT au_fname+' '+ au_lname 'Author Name',
       SUM(ytd_sales * price) Sales
FROM authors
JOIN titleauthor ON authors.au_id = titleauthor.au_id
JOIN titles ON titleauthor.title_id = titles.title_id
GROUP BY authors.au_fname, authors.au_lname
```

OUTPUT

```
Author Name                                      Sales
------------------------------------------------ --------------
Abraham Bennet                                   81859.0500
Reginald Blotchet-Halls                          180397.2000
Cheryl Carson                                    201501.0000
Michel DeFrance                                  66515.5400
Innes del Castillo                               40619.6800
Ann Dull                                         81900.0000
Marjorie Green                                   137837.8300
Burt Gringlesby                                  61384.0500
Sheryl Hunter                                    81900.0000
etc.
```

There! Now I don't have to sit in front of a $3,000 computer adding up rows with a $2 calculator!

First, I replaced the Name alias with 'Author Name' to make the legend more explanatory; because spaces are significant in SQL, I had to put single quotation marks around it to tell SQL server that both words were included in the alias. Next, to tell SQL Server to sum the money totals, I wrapped the ytd_sales * price expression in a SUM aggregate function. Finally, I added the GROUP BY clause at the end to tell SQL Server to combine rows with the same author names.

As a result, SQL Server sorts the rows before returning them, and then combines them on the columns in the GROUP BY list, at the same time performing the calculations requested with the aggregate functions. In the end, Marjorie gets just one line with the sum of all her books.

SQL Server needs to know all the details about how to combine rows in the result. Therefore, when you use GROUP BY, you must put all columns into the GROUP BY list that are not enclosed in an aggregate function, even if the data will not produce duplicates on another column.

HAVING eliminates rows *after* the grouping step in much the same way WHERE eliminates them from the rows returned from SELECT. For example, if you follow the GROUP BY in the previous example with HAVING and a criterion, you get these results:

INPUT

```
SELECT au_fname+' '+ au_lname 'Author Name',
       SUM(ytd_sales * price) Sales
FROM authors
JOIN titleauthor ON authors.au_id = titleauthor.au_id
JOIN titles ON titleauthor.title_id = titles.title_id
GROUP BY authors.au_fname, authors.au_lname
HAVING SUM(ytd_sales * price) > 100000
```

OUTPUT

```
Author Name                                        Sales
-------------------------------------------------- --------------
Reginald Blotchet-Halls                            180397.2000
Cheryl Carson                                      201501.0000
Marjorie Green                                     137837.8300
Michael O'Leary                                    107702.2500

(4 row(s) affected)
```

Note that you can't use the alias in the HAVING; you must use the expression you used in the SELECT list to produce the value.

ORDER BY sorts the output by the columns you specify. To sort in reverse ("descending") order, use the DESC keyword.

COMPUTE [BY] creates subtotals of data in the output rows, again, after all the summarizing and sorting in the GROUP BY and ORDER BY calculations. To simply summarize the sales shown in the previous queries, modify the statement so:

INPUT

```
SELECT au_fname+' '+ au_lname 'Author Name',
       SUM(ytd_sales * price) 'Sales'
FROM authors
JOIN titleauthor ON authors.au_id = titleauthor.au_id
JOIN titles ON titleauthor.title_id = titles.title_id
GROUP BY au_fname, au_lname
ORDER BY 'Author Name'
COMPUTE SUM( SUM(ytd_sales * price) )
```

OUTPUT

```
Author Name                                        Sales
-------------------------------------------------- --------------
Abraham Bennet                                     81859.0500
Akiko Yokomoto                                     61384.0500
.
.
Sheryl Hunter                                      81900.0000
Stearns MacFeather                                 54414.4500
Sylvia Panteley                                    7856.2500

                                                   sum
                                                   =============
                                                   1475358.610
```

This statement returns the same *rowset* as before, but then reports the sum of all the sales at the end.

COMPUTE BY is a little odd in that it requires the data to be sorted, so you must use the ORDER BY clause to prepare the data for it. For your trouble, it will calculate on rows of data in a similar manner as GROUP BY, except it will show you the source data as well. The following SQL will compute subtotals by author, instead of adding up the whole list:

INPUT

```
SELECT au_fname+' '+ au_lname 'Author Name', ytd_sales * price
FROM authors
JOIN titleauthor ON authors.au_id = titleauthor.au_id
JOIN titles ON titleauthor.title_id = titles.title_id
ORDER BY 'Author Name'
COMPUTE SUM( ytd_sales * price ) BY 'Author Name'
```

OUTPUT

```
Author Name
------------------------------------------------ --------------
Abraham Bennet                                   81859.0500

                                                 sum

                                                 81859.0500
   .
   .
Marjorie Green                                   81859.0500
Marjorie Green                                   55978.7800

                                                 sum
                                                 ===============
                                                 137837.8300
   .

   .
Sylvia Panteley                                  7856.2500

                                                 sum
                                                 ===============
                                                 7856.2500
```

The balance of the SELECT statement, those clauses I demonstrated here, can quickly create reports and summaries directly from the database. Though you can achieve similar results with reporting software packages, they cannot match the interactivity of exploration with SQL.

Correlating Data with Subqueries

The queries you've seen so far have had explicit criteria linking tables and specifying rows to retrieve. This is a common need, but there are also situations in which you will not have the data on hand that you need in your search. Many times, for example, the criteria you want to use to limit rows in the WHERE portion of your SELECT will come from some other table or query. On several occasions, I've seen someone hunched over a computer with a database report in hand, looking for information in the database by querying on information in the report—which also came from that database. There has to be a better way to do it, right?

Because I spent so long leading up to it, you know I'm going to supply one. The knight in shining armor is the *subquery*: a query that you execute inside your main query. Anywhere you can place an expression in your query, you can use another query instead. For example, in the query to retrieve sales totals from the previous section, suppose you want to give an award to the authors with best-selling books, those with above average sales. You could query the average from the table, and then use it in the WHERE clause of a second select, but this wastes time and energy, particularly if your query is issued in a program or ASP script that you write. Instead, where you would place the value in the WHERE clause, replace it with the query for the average, in parentheses:

INPUT

```
SELECT CONVERT( varchar(25),
       au_fname + ' ' + au_lname ) Name,
       price*ytd_sales Sales, Title
FROM authors
JOIN titleauthor ON authors.au_id = titleauthor.au_id
JOIN titles ON titleauthor.title_id = titles.title_id
WHERE price * ytd_sales > (
       SELECT AVG(price*ytd_sales)
       FROM titles
)
ORDER BY Sales DESC
```

OUTPUT

```
Name                         Sales             Title
-------------------------    --------------    ------------------
Cheryl Carson                201501.0000       But Is It User Frien
Reginald Blotchet-Halls      180397.2000       Fifty Years in Bucki
```

Ann Dull	81900.0000	Secrets of Silicon V
Sheryl Hunter	81900.0000	Secrets of Silicon V
Marjorie Green	81859.0500	The Busy Executive's
Abraham Bennet	81859.0500	The Busy Executive's
Dean Straight	81859.0500	Straight Talk About
Johnson White	81399.2800	Prolonged Data Depri
Michel DeFrance	66515.5400	The Gourmet Microwav
Anne Ringer	66515.5400	The Gourmet Microwav

So there are your best-sellers, ordered by descending sales (note that I truncated the output rows to keep them from wrapping).

You can also refer to the main query (the *outer* query) from the subquery (the *inner* query). This form of statement, called a *correlated subquery*, is rather rare because most operations for which you would consider a correlated subquery can be accomplished using joins; if there is a relationship with which to correlate the inner and outer queries, it can often be simplified with a join instead. Correlated subqueries are useful mainly where there is only a loose relationship between tables that must be compared for selection.

For example, the following statement retrieves the authors whose names match the beginning of another person's name in the authors table:

INPUT

```
SELECT au_fname, au_lname
FROM Authors au
WHERE EXISTS (
    SELECT au_id
    FROM Authors au2
    WHERE au2.au_lname LIKE au.au_lname + '%'
      AND au2.au_id <> au.au_id
)
```

OUTPUT

```
au_fname              au_lname
-------------------   ----------------------------------------
Marjorie              Green
Albert                Ringer
Anne                  Ringer
```

To refer to the outer query, you have to alias any common tables, as shown. The important thing to remember when using a subquery is that the inner statement will execute once for each row in the outer one; therefore, when your inner statement is executed, it can refer to the values in the current row in the outer query. In this example, the outer query selects all the authors rows, and then for each one, executes the inner query. The inner SELECT queries for any other authors with similar names; the EXISTS function returns true if any matches are found (that is, if the inner SELECT returns any rows). The second criterion in the WHERE clause of the inner select, au2.au_id <> au.au_id, keeps it from matching the same author that is current in the outer statement.

Summary

In this, the last "querying" lesson, you have learned the remainder of the SQL SELECT statement. Close on its heels were subqueries: queries you can nest within queries to perform more complex analysis. With the intervening discussion, I think you'll agree with my introduction of SQL as a deceptively simple language. Given some ingenuity (and practice), the results you can produce with queries are amazing.

LESSON 13
More SQL: Defining Data

In this lesson, you'll move beyond using existing databases and learn to create your own.

To this point, you've been working with databases without worrying about how the database got there. In this lesson, I'll show you something of how SQL Server stores your data, and how to create, modify, and delete objects in the database.

Databases, Files, and File Groups

Each database you work with has at least two subdivisions: the data storage and the transaction log. The data storage is where the database stores all the objects in your database, including table definitions, table data, view definitions, stored procedures, logins, everything. The transaction log stores everything you do to the database, with a few exceptions.

The Transaction Log

In Lesson 4, "Adding and Changing Data," I showed you how to use a transaction to test a statement without applying the changes it made to the database. The underlying mechanics of doing this are conceptually pretty simple. When you begin a statement (such as an UPDATE) that will change data in the database, the server creates a new transaction entry in the transaction log. Before it makes any changes, it writes all the changes it is about to make into that transaction record, with any information necessary to undo, or *roll back*, the changes. Only after the transaction data is stored in the transaction log will it make the changes to the data in the database tables. When the changes are completed, it marks the transaction entry in the transaction log as *committed*, or complete and permanent.

In this manner, the database preserves data integrity even if catastrophe befalls it in the middle of a change. If the power fails when it is in the middle of writing the transaction to the transaction log, the server will simply erase the transaction when it next boots. If the failure comes when it is changing the data in the database tables (the second step), it can use the information in the transaction log to roll back the changes and return the database to its previous state. In the example in Lesson 4, I directed the database to roll back the changes, that is, undo what I had done and bring the data back that was deleted.

Data Storage

A database is stored in one or more file groups, each of which uses one or more data files on your hard disk to hold the data from your database (see Figure 13.1).

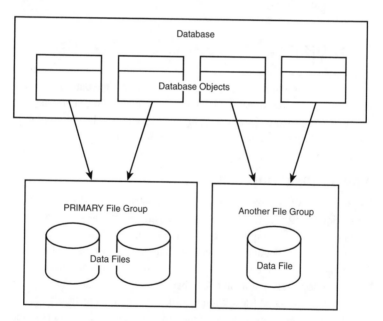

FIGURE 13.1 The relationship of databases, file groups, and files.

When you create a database in SQL Server, you must provide it the names of the files it will use for the database and transaction log. These will be created in the PRIMARY file group and used to store both the data and information that describes the database as a whole.

SQL Server uses the model database to initialize new databases you create. Model is set up when you install SQL Server to contain the basics needed by any database you might create on the server. Thereafter, whenever you create a new database, SQL Server initializes it by copying all objects in model to your new database. A database administrator can also use this feature to include administrator-defined objects in all databases. All objects the administrator creates in model will be duplicated in any new databases created thereafter.

After you create the database, you can create additional data files in the PRIMARY file group if, for example, you have multiple disks on which to store data. SQL Server will distribute the data among the files in a file group. If the files are each on different devices, this balances the load across different disks.

There are many other instances in which you might wish to store data in different locations, most of them dependent upon the problem you are trying to solve and the server hardware you have available. One that is not, however, is selection of storage for the transaction log. If possible, you should store the transaction log on a different device from the database files themselves. I'll speak more of this in Lesson 18, "Keeping Your Server Safe."

Data Definition Language Commands

The Data Definition Language (DDL) commands you'll see here are CREATE, ALTER, and DROP. You'll use these commands to manipulate most *schema* objects in the database.

 Schema   This term refers to the design of the database at a particular level. In this lesson, I am referring to the *physical schema*, which includes the files, tables, relations, stored procedures, indices, defaults, triggers, and views in the physical database design.

CREATE

CREATE is used to create new databases and schema objects in databases. Its syntax varies depending on the object you are creating. Table 13.1 shows various forms of CREATE. I'll discuss here only the forms of CREATE that I don't describe in other lessons.

TABLE 13.1 The Many Ways to Employ CREATE

Object	CREATE Method
DATABASE	CREATE DATABASE *dbname* ON *filespec* [, *filespec* ...] [, *filegroup* ...] [LOG ON *filespec* [, *filespec* ...] [FOR { LOAD ¦ ATTACH }]
DEFAULT	CREATE DEFAULT *defaultname* AS *constant*
INDEX	CREATE [UNIQUE] [CLUSTERED ¦ NONCLUSTERED] INDEX *indexname* ON *tableref*(*colref* [, *colref* ...]) (see Lesson 11)
PROCEDURE	CREATE PROC[EDURE] *procname* AS *sql* (see Lesson 14)
RULE	CREATE RULE *name* AS *ruleexp*
SCHEMA	CREATE SCHEMA AUTHORIZATION *owner* *ddl_or_dcl_stmt* [*ddl_or_dcl_stmt* ...]

TABLE	CREATE TABLE *tablename*
	(
	    col_or_const_def
	    [, *col_or_const_def* ...]
	)
	[ON *filegroup* [DEFAULT]]
	[TEXTIMAGE_ON *filegroup* [DEFAULT]]

TRIGGER	CREATE TRIGGER *trigname* ON *tableref* FOR *operation* AS *sql* (see Lesson 15)

Object	CREATE Method
VIEW	CREATE VIEW *viewname* [(*colname* [, *colname* ...])] AS *sql* (see Lesson 16)

Databases

Creating a database creates the files you specify, formats the data file to prepare it for storing data, and then copies the model database into it. When you create a database, you must at least provide a name for it (*dbname*) and name at least one data file to hold the database.

The *filespec* in the CREATE DATABASE statement takes the following form:

SYNTAX

```
filespec: ( FILENAME = 'filename'
             [, NAME = logical_name ]
             [, SIZE = n[ KB ¦ MB ] ]
             [, MAXSIZE = n[ KB ¦ MB ] ]
             [, FILEGROWTH = n[ KB ¦ MB ¦ % ] ]
           )
```

You use the *filespec* to specify where to store the database data. If you specify more than one *filespec*, SQL Server will store the start of the database in the first file, and then distribute data among it and the remaining files. Use this mechanism to disperse your database across multiple disks if needed. If you want the primary data file to be other than the first, use the PRIMARY keyword before the *filespec* that you want to be the primary file. Listing 13.1 creates a 5 megabyte database with a 1 megabyte transaction log, which can grow to 10 MB and 5 MB, respectively, in 1 MB increments.

LISTING 13.1   Creating a Database

```
CREATE DATABASE testdb
ON
(
    NAME = test_data,
    FILENAME = 'v:\test.mdf',
    SIZE = 5 MB,
    MAXSIZE = 10 MB,
    FILEGROWTH = 1 MB
)
```

continues

Listing 13.1   Continued

```
LOG ON
(
    NAME = test_log,
    FILENAME = 'w:\test.ldf',
    SIZE = 1 MB,
    MAXSIZE = 5 MB,
    FILEGROWTH = 1 MB
)
```

As shown in Table 13.1, you might also create file groups in the CREATE DATABASE statement; the *filegroup* in the syntax is of the form FILEGROUP *fgname filespec*, in which *fgname* is the name for the file group.

Tables

To create a table, you must tell SQL Server what to name it, what columns and constraints go in it, and optionally what file group to place it in. The *col_or_const_def* in the format is either a column, a computed column, or a table constraint definition. For a column, you provide the name, data type and optionally, an IDENTITY specification. You will also usually include one or more column constraints. Listing 13.2 illustrates creating a parts table to hold inventory information. In the listing, I've spaced the column definitions so the name is in the first column, the type in the second, additional column attributes in the third, and constraints last.

Listing 13.2   Table Definition with Column Constraints and Defaults

```
CREATE TABLE parts
(
    ID        int          IDENTITY( 1, 1 )  PRIMARY KEY,
    name      char(40)                       NOT NULL,
    qty       int                            CONSTRAINT qtyVal
                                                 DEFAULT 0,
    price     money                          NOT NULL,
    description varchar(255)                 NULL,

    value_on_hand AS ( price * qty ),
)
```

Analysis   In Listing 13.2, the ID column is the primary key for the table, and uses an IDENTITY to generate the key values. An IDENTITY column cannot be modified by a query; instead, SQL Server will generate counter values for it when you insert rows. In the example, the numbers in the IDENTITY specification tell SQL Server to start counting at one, and to count by one up.

The name column shows a required field. By placing the NOT NULL constraint on the column, any row insertion on the table, or any modification to an existing row, will be rejected if it will result in a row not having a value in the name column.

The qty column shows how to set a default constraint for the column; in this case, the default quantity will be zero if a row is created without giving the value. This also demonstrates how to name a constraint. The nullability constraints do not get names, but other constraints do; if you don't specify a name for the constraint, SQL Server will dream one up. For clarity, you might want to assign a name yourself. The example names the DEFAULT constraint qtyVal.

The last column, value_on_hand, uses one of the neatest new features of SQL 7: the computed column. You can't modify a computed column—you tell SQL Server how to calculate values for it instead. Whenever you retrieve rows from the parts table, the value_on_hand column will show the result of the calculation parts * qty, or the value of the current inventory. You can only use columns in the same table in the computation, but this still promises to be a handy feature.

Constraints can be defined at the table level as well. Listing 13.3 shows this method.

LISTING 13.3 Creating Table Constraints

```
CREATE TABLE orders
(
   orderNo          int              IDENTITY( 100, 1 ),
   partId      int,
   qty         int,

   CONSTRAINT PK_ORDER_NR PRIMARY KEY( orderNo ),
   CONSTRAINT FK_ORDERS_PARTS FOREIGN KEY( partId )
                          REFERENCES parts( ID ),
   CONSTRAINT ORDER_QTY CHECK( qty > 0 )
)
```

ANALYSIS   The orders table references the parts table to show which part was ordered and contains a CHECK constraint on the qty column to ensure that orders for nothing aren't created.

Miscellaneous

The other statements in the table are shown only for completeness in case you need to look up syntax later. CREATE RULE and CREATE DEFAULT can be used to create defaults and rules (essentially, check constraints) that are stored outside any table and can be applied to multiple tables. This can be useful in large data models, but is easy to get mixed up. For smaller models, you'll do better to keep the definitions with the tables as I've demonstrated.

The CREATE SCHEMA statement is something of an oddball; its main purpose is allowing you to create objects in the same statement that refer to each other. When you create a table with a FOREIGN KEY constraint, the other table and column(s) must exist; if you need to create two tables that reference each other, you must first create the tables, and then use ALTER TABLE to add the constraints. You can create them in a single batch transaction using the CREATE SCHEMA statement, but first think through why you really want to have the tables reference each other. Such *circular dependencies* usually are not the best solution.

ALTER

No matter how careful you are, you'll probably not get everything right when you design your databases. Unfortunately, you often find out what you left out after people are already using the database, and dropping and recreating the objects that need to change is not a popularity-enhancing option. ALTER can be used to change databases, tables, procedures, triggers, and views in the database.

Databases

The only alteration to a database you can make is to add and remove files or file groups, or change their size. To add or modify a file, you use the same syntax for a *filespec* as you do in the CREATE, demonstrated in Listing 13.4.

LISTING 13.4   Adding a Database File

```
ALTER DATABASE testdb
ADD FILE
(
```

```
    NAME = 'testfile2',
    FILENAME = 'v:\testfile2.ndf',
    SIZE = 1 MB,
    MAXSIZE = 10 MB,
    FILEGROWTH = 1 MB
)
```

Modifying a file is the same form, but you supply the name of a file already in the database, and supply the new sizes and growth increment you would like. You can also drop a file, but only if there is no data in it. You can add a file to a specific file group by stating, ADD FILE TO FILEGROUP *fgname*.

To remove the file added in Listing 13.4, you'd execute the following:

```
ALTER DATABASE testdb
REMOVE FILE testfile2
```

Tables

Tables can have columns and constraints added, modified, and removed. To add a constraint or column, use the following statement:

```
ALTER TABLE tablename
ADD { coldef ¦ condef }
```

For adding columns and constraints, *coldef* and *condef* are the descriptions of the column and the constraint, respectively, with the same format as in the CREATE statement. For example, the SQL in Listing 13.5 is equivalent to that in Listing 13.3, but adds the ORDER_QTY constraint after the table is created.

LISTING 13.5   Creating Table Constraints

```
CREATE TABLE orders
(
    orderNo       int              IDENTITY( 100, 1 ),
    partId        int,
    qty           int,

    CONSTRAINT PK_ORDER_NR PRIMARY KEY( orderNo ),
    CONSTRAINT FK_ORDERS_PARTS FOREIGN KEY( partId )
                            REFERENCES parts( ID ),
)

ALTER TABLE orders
ADD CONSTRAINT ORDER_QTY CHECK( qty > 0 )
```

When you add a constraint to the table, you can use a WITH NOCHECK option to stop SQL Server from checking existing columns to see if they match. This is risky business because you cannot be sure then that all data in the table conforms to the constraint, but if you have to, you can.

You can remove a constraint or column with the following command:

```
ALTER TABLE tablename DROP col_or_con_name
```

In this statement, tablename is the table to change and col_or_con_name is the column or constraint to delete.

In rare cases, you might need to change the type or size of a column; for example, if you create a char column for 40 characters, and then discover you need 80 characters instead. The syntax for this form is as follows:

```
ALTER TABLE   tablename
ALTER COLUMN  col_name
              new_type [ ( size_or_scale [, precision] ) ]
              [ NULL ¦ NOT NULL ]
```

You could expand the description column of the parts table with this SQL:

```
ALTER TABLE parts ALTER COLUMN description varchar( 1024 ) NULL
```

Altering columns can be problematic because there are issues of data preservation involved. In general, if the alteration will lose data or cast the integrity of the database into doubt, you will not be able to effect a change. The only modification you can assume you will be able to perform is the one shown: expanding the column's type to a larger equivalent type.

DROP

DROP is the DDL equivalent of DML's DELETE, and it's just as complex. To delete a database object, you use the command DROP obj_type object_name, where obj_type is the sort of object you want to be rid of, and object_name is the name of the specific one. Listing 13.6 shows some common DROPs.

LISTING 13.6   Example DROP Statements

```
DROP INDEX parts.partNameIdx
DROP TABLE orders
DROP DATABASE testdb
```

In general, you can drop any of the schema objects you've seen. For an index, you have to supply the name of the table it is on. You cannot drop files or file groups directly, as you might remember; for these, you must use the ALTER DATABASE statement.

The Sample Application's Tables

As promised, now that you have seen the syntax for all the components, Listing 13.7 shows the SQL to create the tables used in the ASP sample you saw in Lesson 10, "An Interactive Web Application." This SQL was created by SQL Server out of the database.

LISTING 13.7   Guestbook Application Tables

```
 1: CREATE TABLE [dbo].[Activity] (
 2:     [Name] [varchar] (20) NOT NULL
 3: ) ON [PRIMARY]
 4:
 5: CREATE TABLE [dbo].[Site] (
 6:     [URL] [varchar] (100) NOT NULL ,
 7:     [Description] [varchar] (2000) NOT NULL
 8: ) ON [PRIMARY]
 9:
10: CREATE TABLE [dbo].[Person] (
11:     [Name] [char] (100) NOT NULL ,
12:     [Email] [varchar] (100) NOT NULL ,
13:     [FaveSiteURL] [varchar] (100) NOT NULL ,
14:     [ActivityName] [varchar] (20) NOT NULL
15: ) ON [PRIMARY]
16:
17: CREATE TABLE [dbo].[Comment] (
18:     [PersonName] [char] (100) NOT NULL ,
19:     [CommentText] [text] NOT NULL
20: ) ON [PRIMARY] TEXTIMAGE_ON [PRIMARY]
21:
22: ALTER TABLE [dbo].[Activity] WITH NOCHECK ADD
23:     CONSTRAINT [PK_Activity] PRIMARY KEY   NONCLUSTERED
24:     (
25:         [Name]
26:     )  ON [PRIMARY]
27:
28: ALTER TABLE [dbo].[Site] WITH NOCHECK ADD
29:     CONSTRAINT [PK_Site] PRIMARY KEY   NONCLUSTERED
30:     (
```

continues

LISTING 13.7 Continued

```
31:            [URL]
32:        )   ON [PRIMARY]
33:
34: ALTER TABLE [dbo].[Person] WITH NOCHECK ADD
35:        CONSTRAINT [PK_Person] PRIMARY KEY   NONCLUSTERED
36:        (
37:            [Name]
38:        )   ON [PRIMARY]
39:
40: ALTER TABLE [dbo].[Person] ADD
41:        CONSTRAINT [FK_Person_Activity1] FOREIGN KEY
42:        (
43:            [ActivityName]
44:        ) REFERENCES [dbo].[Activity] (
45:            [Name]
46:        ),
47:        CONSTRAINT [FK_Person_Site] FOREIGN KEY
48:        (
49:            [FaveSiteURL]
50:        ) REFERENCES [dbo].[Site] (
51:            [URL]
52:        )
53:
54: ALTER TABLE [dbo].[Comment] ADD
55:        CONSTRAINT [FK_Comment_Person] FOREIGN KEY
56:        (
57:            [PersonName]
58:        ) REFERENCES [dbo].[Person] (
59:            [Name]
60:        )
```

ANALYSIS When generating scripts from existing objects, SQL Server uses the ALTER TABLE syntax (lines 22, 28, 34, 40, and 54) to describe the constraints on the tables. This is probably because they are stored separately from the table in the database.

An additional oddity is the script's use of the NONCLUSTERED (lines 23, 29, and 35) and NOCHECK (lines 22, 28, and 34) options on the primary keys. Though these might be needed on tables containing data, this script was created all at once to create the tables and the constraints. It's nothing a little search and replace won't fix, but it's strange.

Summary

In this lesson, you rounded out your database skills with the common DDL statements used on SQL Server and saw several examples of how to use them. You can now create tables, relationships, indices, and the databases to hold them, use Microsoft Office to manipulate the data, and build Web sites to provide the data to others. Not bad for a few hours' reading!

In the next three lessons, you're going to see the remainder of the schema objects I'm going to describe: stored procedure, triggers, and views. You can use these objects to manage the integrity and usability of your databases.

LESSON 14

Storing SQL in the Database

This lesson teaches you about stored procedures, a powerful tool for increasing the maintainability and performance of your applications.

Now you'll look at the method SQL Server provides for storing SQL in the database in precompiled objects called *stored procedures*. When you create a stored procedure, you create a set of SQL statements that can be executed by name from other SQL.

Several important factors give rise to the use of stored procedures. First, creating a database creates a record of some number of entities; in the model you construct, the things that can be done to those entities should be fairly well defined. The example of a transfer between bank accounts comes to mind, where the source account must be debited and the target credited, all in a manner that ensures the rules are followed. If you write a stored procedure to accomplish the transfer, and require the stored procedure be used to accomplish the action, you know that it will be done correctly every time—you don't have to rely on the client applications to get it right.

Second, stored procedures are just plain faster than issuing several SQL statements from your client program or script. As you recall, each query from your program has to be parsed, planned, and executed when the database receives it. Though SQL Server does a good job of optimizing this process, when you call a stored procedure, it has to do a lot less work to prepare everything.

Third and last, there are some things that you can't do well, or at all, from the client program. Some features of SQL that are readily available from a stored procedure require you to write client code using techniques that aren't necessarily obvious. Stored procedures let you write the SQL to get the job done without researching the arcana of your client software.

Unfortunately, when you use stored procedures you sacrifice portability. In fact, I have never worked with an RDBMS that implemented the

SQL92 specification for stored procedures. The dialect of SQL spoken by SQL Server 7, called *Transact-SQL*, provides a powerful procedural programming facility, as this lesson will show you, but procedures you write will usually not work with other database servers.

Creating Stored Procedures

You use the following command to create a stored procedure:

```
CREATE PROC[EDURE] procname
    [ @paramname paramtype [= default_value][OUTPUT] [,
@paramname etc. ...] ]
    [ WITH [RECOMPILE] [[,] ENCRYPTION ] ]
AS
    SQLstmt [ SQLstmt ... ]
```

For an example, as often as you've used the query to retrieve the authors and books they've written, you can probably type it in your sleep. The following stores it in a procedure so you don't have to:

```
CREATE PROCEDURE show_authors_books
AS

SELECT au_fname + ' ' + au_lname 'Author Name', title 'Title'
FROM authors
JOIN titleauthor ON titleauthor.au_id = authors.au_id
JOIN titles ON titles.title_id = titleauthor.title_id
```

When you execute this SQL, SQL Server stores the SQL statement after the AS in the database with the name show_authors. You can execute the procedure in Query Analyzer after it's created:

```
EXEC show_authors_books
```

```
Author Name            Title
---------------------  -------------------------------
Abraham Bennet         The Busy Executive's Database Guide
Reginald Blotchet-Halls Fifty Years in Buckingham Palace Ki
```

```
Cheryl Carson        But Is It User Friendly?
Michel DeFrance      The Gourmet Microwave
Innes del Castillo   Silicon Valley Gastronomic Treats
etc.
```

I used the EXEC keyword for demonstration purposes; EXEC is the Transact-SQL statement you use to invoke a stored procedure. If the stored procedure call (invocation) is the only statement in your query, you can call a procedure by just typing its name and any necessary parameters. At any other time, you must use EXEC.

Using Variables and Cursors

Stored procedures are something like mini-programs that you store in the database. You can use multiple statements in a stored procedure if you want to perform several operations in one setting; for example, updating multiple tables. You can create variables as well (similar to the variables you used in ASP scripts) except you *must* declare variables before using them in SQL, and you have to state what type they are when you declare them.

You can create and manipulate *cursors* in your stored procedure, too. Cursors are similar to the Recordset variables you used with ADO, in that they present a moving window across rows of data. Cursors have a lot more utility than Recordsets, though; you can control retrievals and updates completely with a server cursor. Recordsets, because they must be able to work with any server database, can't provide that degree of control directly. Cursors don't hold the data to which they provide access, though, so you have to provide variables outside of the cursor that will hold the columns in the current row.

It's hard to show variables without showing cursors, so I'm going to use both in an example of a procedure that uses a cursor to move across the authors table, and then gives each contract author a well-deserved five percent increase in their royalty percentage. Listing 14.1 shows the code.

LISTING 14.1   Stored Procedure to Give Authors a Raise

```
1: CREATE PROCEDURE AuthorsRaise
2: AS
3:
4: -- declare local variables I'll use to work with data
5: DECLARE @contract bit, @au_id id
6:
```

```
 7:  -- declare the cursor I'll use to scan the authors table
 8:  DECLARE au_cursor CURSOR
 9:      FOR SELECT au_id, contract FROM authors
10:
11:  -- open cursor and get the first row
12:  OPEN au_cursor
13:  FETCH NEXT FROM au_cursor INTO @au_id, @contract
14:
15:  -- do this as long as there are more rows in the cursor
16:  WHILE @@FETCH_STATUS = 0
17:  BEGIN
18:
19:      --if the author is contracted, then give a raise
20:      IF @contract <> 0
21:      BEGIN
22:          -- this is just normal SQL
23:          UPDATE titleauthor
24:          SET royaltyper = royaltyper + 5
25:          WHERE au_id = @au_id
26:              AND royaltyper <= 95
27:      END
28:
29:      --get the next row; if no more exist, @@FETCH_STATUS
30:      --will become negative, and I'll exit the WHILE
31:      FETCH NEXT FROM au_cursor INTO @au_id, @contract
32:  END
33:
34:  CLOSE au_cursor
```

ANALYSIS   I'll walk you through this SQL the same way I have with other programming demonstrations I've shown you.

The first line, the CREATE PROCEDURE AuthorsRaise AS tells SQL Server you are creating a stored procedure and what to name it. *Everything* after the AS becomes a part of the code in your procedure; because of that, you can't execute any SQL in a query that creates a stored procedure that you don't want to be part of the procedure.

The first DECLARE (line 5) tells SQL Server I'm going to work with two variables in the procedure, @contract and @au_id. In ASP, you didn't have to declare variables if you didn't want to, and you couldn't assign a type to them even if you did. In a stored procedure, though, you have to declare the variable *and* its type, and if you try to store data into it of a type other than what you declared, your procedure will fail. Variables in a procedure are named starting with the at sign (@) followed by a normal SQL name. SQL Server maintains a number of system variables for you that you can check for various pieces of status information; these are prefixed with two at signs (@@).

The next DECLARE (lines 8–9) creates a cursor that I'll use to work with the authors table. Remember, like a Recordset, you can use a cursor to scan the rows in a table or query. When you declare the cursor, you provide the SQL, whether a table reference or a more complicated query, that will provide the cursor's rows. In this procedure, the cursor will SELECT the au_id and contract columns from authors. I'm going to move this cursor across all the authors, and for each contract author, use the au_id to update the royaltyper royalty percentage in titleauthor.

The OPEN statement in line 12 tells SQL Server to set up au_cursor for use. I then retrieve the first row into local variables using the FETCH NEXT command in line 13. You use FETCH to retrieve the values from the current record in the cursor into your variables. FETCH NEXT moves the cursor to the next row before retrieving values. The variables you supply must be the same type (or an equivalent) and in the same order as the columns in the cursor's SELECT, and you must supply a variable for every column in the cursor.

The WHILE statement (line 16) does the work in this procedure. It's similar to that in ASP, but instead of using a WEND to end the block that gets repeated, SQL uses BEGIN to start the block and END to end it. In this procedure the condition is whether the variable @@FETCH_STATUS is zero; this system variable is set by SQL Server each time you FETCH data from a cursor, to zero (for success) or a negative value (some error occurred, or there's no more data).

Within the WHILE, the code is obvious. If the author is a contract author, as indicated in the @contract variable (line 20), the UPDATE in line 23 adds five percent to the royalty percentage, unless that would put the author over 100 percent (the folks already getting 96 to 99 percent are out of luck). The FETCH at line 31 gets the next row from the cursor.

When everything is done, the CLOSE statement at line 34 tells SQL Server you're done with the cursor, so SQL Server can free up the resources used by it.

Cursor Details

You use a cursor over some length of time that you are retrieving data. Your procedure takes a few seconds (or a few minutes or even hours) to execute, but *you are not the only one using the database*. Between the time that you open the cursor and the time that you finish working with the data it refers to, someone might change the data you are inspecting. You have two questions to answer, then: While you're looking at the data with your cursor, are people allowed to change the data? If they are, do you want to see the changes?

The answers to these questions describe the *locking* and *isolation* behavior you need. If you *lock* the data your cursor retrieves, you prohibit anyone from making any updates to it. This is the safest behavior because whatever exists when you start working with the data will still be the same when you're done. However, when you're running a large update against a database, this also means that your users are going to be waiting until you're done.

In SQL Server, your cursor will have the same isolation and locking behavior as your overall session. In a default installation, this produces a dynamic cursor with optimistic locking; in other words, the data are not locked on retrieval, and you see whatever changes are made to the source data tables immediately.

To ignore changes made to the data while you're working with your cursor, declare the cursor as INSENSITIVE, as in the following:

```
DECLARE au_cursor INSENSITIVE CURSOR
    FOR SELECT au_id, contract FROM authors
```

Use this with care—this creates a *static* cursor that works with a copy of the rows in the tables, as they were when you opened it. With large, volatile data sets, this can hog valuable disk and memory space.

Usually, the default or static cursors will suffice. If you need more advanced behavior, look at the SET TRANSACTION ISOLATION LEVEL statement and the "Cursors" topic in Books Online's Transact SQL Reference. For a quick, but technical, discussion of SQL Server lock behavior, search for "Understanding locking in SQL Server" in the Search tab of Books Online.

Managing Procedures

When SQL Server stores your procedure, it stores the SQL itself in the syscomments table in your database. You and other users on the database can retrieve the text in the procedure with the system stored procedure sp_helptext *procname*, where *procname* is the procedure's name. You can remove this capability by including the WITH ENCRYPTION option in the CREATE PROCEDURE statement. This option scrambles the procedure's text in the database so no one, including you, can read it. If you choose this option, make sure you save the SQL to create your procedures! If you don't, you'll never see it again.

I don't advise that you encrypt stored procedures when you're developing them; often, your procedure won't do what you want it to do the first time you write it, if it's at all complex, and you might want to change its function or output. You modify a procedure using the ALTER PROCEDURE statement, which has exactly the same syntax as the CREATE PROCEDURE statement. ALTER PROCEDURE replaces the procedure you name in the database with new text or options. You might use it to turn on encryption for a procedure that currently is not encrypted, for example. A nice feature of ALTER PROCEDURE is that it does not affect any permissions or dependencies that apply to the procedure.

Delete a stored procedure with DROP PROCEDURE *procname*.

Passing Parameters

Just as with ASP scripts, you'll often want to provide data to a procedure that it can use to do its job. *Passing parameters* to the procedure requires you to declare the parameters when you create the procedure, and then provide the values when you execute it. Parameters are named with the same @*varname* syntax as variables and come between the *procname* and any procedure options in the CREATE statement. Listing 14.2 shows a procedure to add a part to the parts table from Lesson 13, using values you supply.

LISTING 14.2   Stored Procedure to Add a Part

```
CREATE PROC AddPart
    @part_name char(40),
    @part_qty int,
    @part_price money,
    @part_descr varchar(255) = NULL
```

AS

```
-- create the new record
INSERT parts(name, qty, price, description)
VALUES(@part_name, @part_qty, @part_price, @part_descr)
```

ANALYSIS In this example, there are four parameters to the procedure. When you execute the procedure, you will have to supply at least the first three. This makes sense because these three values are required in the parts table. The fourth supplies a *default* value; if you only supply the first three parameters when you call the procedure, SQL Server will fill in the fourth parameter with the default, NULL in this case. If you supply a value when you call the procedure, that value will be used instead.

You can demonstrate this procedure with the following SQL in Query Analyzer:

INPUT

```
SELECT * FROM parts

EXEC AddPart 'Whatsit', 7, $49.99

SELECT * FROM parts
```

This shows what is already in the table, adds a part, and then shows the table again so you can see the result. The output will look like the following (I've cut off the output that would run off the page):

OUTPUT

```
 1: ID            name               qty          price ...
 2: ----------    ----------------   ---------    ---------
 3:
 4: (0 row(s) affected)
 5:
 6:
 7: (1 row(s) affected)
 8:
 9: ID            name               qty          price ...
10: ----------    ----------------   ----------   ---------
11: 8             Whatsit            7            49.9900
12:
13: (1 row(s) affected)
```

ANALYSIS No rows are returned from the first SELECT because there are no rows in the table yet. When the procedure executes to insert the row, one row

is created, producing the middle report of 1 row(s) affected (line 7). The
last SELECT demonstrates that the row was inserted successfully by retrieving
it from the previously empty table (lines 9–13).

The values provided after the procedure name in the EXEC filled in the
parameters in the procedure's parameter list in order (refer to Listing 14.2
for their definitions). If you prefer, you can explicitly state which parameters receive which data by assigning each parameter directly in the procedure call. The following is functionally the same as the previous example,
even though I list the parameters backward:

```
exec AddPart @part_price = $49.99, @part_qty = 7,
             @part_name = 'Whatsit'
```

Returning Results

If you need to return information from a procedure, you have two options.
A procedure can have a result set just like a normal SQL statement, the
format of which you can control. On the other hand, you can declare parameters to be OUTPUT parameters, meaning that the procedure can assign a
value to them that is available to the SQL that called the procedure.

Result Sets

You saw an example of a procedure returning a result set in the first example, which returned the authors and all their books. This result set can be
used as the source for a cursor, as the data for an ASP Recordset, or anywhere else a result set is expected. Unfortunately, client applications will
usually see a result set for every statement you execute in the procedure that
produces one of those pesky row(s) affected messages. To keep this from
occurring, you can use the SET NOCOUNT statement to turn them off, and then
SELECT explicitly the results you want to go back to the client.

Listing 14.3 shows the AddPart procedure altered to send only the new part
number back to the client, by selecting the @@IDENTITY value. (This variable
holds the value inserted into the last new row with an IDENTITY column.)

LISTING 14.3   Stored Procedure Returning a Result Set

```
1: ALTER PROC AddPart
2:      @part_name char(40),
3:      @part_qty int,
4:      @part_price money,
```

```
 5:        @part_descr varchar(255) = NULL
 6: AS
 7:        -- turn off record counting
 8:        SET NOCOUNT ON
 9:
10:        -- create the new record
11:        INSERT parts( name, qty, price, description )
12:        VALUES( @part_name, @part_qty, @part_price,
13:                   @part_descr )
14:
15:        -- show the new identifier as the result set
16:        -- from this procedure
17:        SELECT @@IDENTITY AS 'NewPartID'
18:
19:        -- turn record counting back on
20:        SET NOCOUNT OFF
```

ANALYSIS This uses the ALTER PROC statement to change the procedure because it already exists in the database. The SET NOCOUNT statements at lines 8 and 20 stop the messages as I discussed, and then line 17's SELECT @@IDENTITY sends one row back to the client, with a single column called NewPartID. If you stored the result into a Recordset called rs in ASP, the part number for the new part would be available as rs("NewPartID") or rs(0).

OUTPUT Parameters

An alternative is to use OUTPUT parameters (or *out parameters*). This is most useful when you are calling a stored procedure from another stored procedure. Out parameters can be any type, including cursors, but must be marked in both the procedure's parameter list and the calling statement as OUTPUT parameters. The called procedure assigns the returned value to the parameter as it would to any variable, but when the procedure finishes executing, the caller can use the value.

Listing 14.4 shows the AddPart procedure modified to use an out parameter instead of a result set.

LISTING 14.4 Stored Procedure Returning an Out Parameter

```
1: CREATE PROC AddPart2
2:        @part_name char(40),
3:        @part_qty int,
```

continues

Listing 14.4   Continued

```
 4:        @part_price money,
 5:        @new_part_id int OUTPUT,
 6:        @part_descr varchar(255) = NULL
 7: AS
 8:        -- turn off record counting
 9:        SET NOCOUNT ON
10:
11:        -- create the new record
12:        INSERT parts( name, qty, price, description )
13:        VALUES( @part_name, @part_qty, @part_price,
14:                @part_descr )
15:
16:        -- place the return value in the out parameter
17:        SELECT @new_part_id = @@IDENTITY
18:
19:        -- turn record counting back on
20:        SET NOCOUNT OFF
```

Analysis The important items are the parameter list (lines 5[nd]6), where
I've added the new_part_id parameter, and SELECT @new_part_id =
@@IDENTITY (line 17), which places the value of the system variable into
the out parameter.

You could execute the modified procedure from another procedure in this
manner:

```
DECLARE @partId int
EXEC AddPart2 'Whatsit', 7, $49.99, @partId OUTPUT
```

After the procedure executes, the @partId variable holds the new part
number.

Summary

This lesson showed you the essence of using stored procedures to store business rules and common functions as database objects. You covered creating
and modifying stored procedures, and how to pass information into and out
from them.

You can use stored procedures to boost both the reliability and performance of your database, and reduce the amount of code needed in your
client applications, but you gain efficiency at the price of portability. Next,
you're going to look at a special kind of stored procedure, called a *trigger*,
which you can use for finer control over changes to your data.

LESSON 15

Controlling How Changes Are Made

In this lesson, you'll learn about a special kind of stored procedure, a trigger, that you can use to control how users change data in your database.

The data in your database is often subject to interlocking rules that govern whether the data "make sense." In addition to low-level referential needs (foreign keys must refer to valid primary keys), higher level rules must be obeyed if the information in your database is going to be realistic.

For example, in the parts table, the qty column that indicates inventory level must not be negative, unless you've entered a singularity and Scotty is busily modifying plasma conduits. In the pubs database, the ytd_sales in titles should reflect the same totals as the sum of individual sales in sales for this year.

Data verification needs range from basic data type validation to abstract business rules the information must conform to. SQL Server provides a layered set of tools for ensuring data quality, including

- Column types

- Declarative referential integrity

- Other column and table constraints

- Triggers

The first three mechanisms have severe restrictions on their use; the last, triggers, picks up where the others leave off.

Working with Triggers

A trigger is a very close cousin to a stored procedure. The syntax for creating them and the SQL you write them in are very similar, but triggers have a very different context and connotation. Rather than being executed by a client on command, a trigger is executed by SQL Server when a particular modification takes place on a table's data. You can write triggers to validate the modification, update other data, or nearly anything else you can do with SQL.

When it is created, a trigger is associated to a table and one or more of the DML statements that change data in a table: UPDATE, INSERT, and DELETE. Thereafter, whenever the associated DML executes against the table, the trigger will execute ("fire," in database parlance). You can have multiple triggers defined on a table, even on the same operation on that table, so you have plenty of flexibility.

 Caution Don't go hog-wild with triggers. Though there is very little built-in overhead involved with triggers, they are executed against every associated operation on their table. If the trigger performs any resource-intensive operations, it can quickly bring your server to its knees if you don't plan ahead.

Creating a Trigger

The following shows the basic syntax for a trigger:

```
CREATE TRIGGER trigname
ON tableref
    [ WITH ENCRYPTION ]
FOR { [UPDATE] [[,]INSERT] [[,]DELETE] }
AS
    [ IF UPDATE( columnref )
        [ { AND ¦ OR } UPDATE( columnref ) ... ] ]
    SQLstmt [ SQLstmt ... ]
```

The tableref is the table to which the trigger will be attached, and FOR ... specifies which operations will fire the trigger. On UPDATE and INSERT triggers, the IF UPDATE... statement can be used to narrow the focus of the trigger to firing only if particular *columns* in the table are updated or inserted; this statement is meaningless on a DELETE trigger, so it is not allowed.

For example, suppose you wanted to audit updates to the authors table into a table defined as the following:

```
CREATE TABLE auditlog
(
    userName   varchar(40),
    operation  varchar(10),
    optime     smalldatetime,
    object     varchar(255)
)
```

The log will store the user making the change, the operation (type of change), the time it was made, and the object that was changed. You could create the trigger in Listing 15.1 on the authors table to record the updates.

LISTING 15.1 Audit Trigger on Authors

```
CREATE TRIGGER author_update_audit
ON authors
FOR UPDATE
AS
    INSERT auditlog( userName, operation, optime, object )
            VALUES( current_user, 'UPDATE', current_
                    timestamp, 'authors' )
```

If you create this trigger and the auditlog table, insert the venerable example author with the following SQL:

```
INSERT authors
VALUES( '123-45-6789', 'Jones', 'Smith', '123 456-7890',
        '123 Main St.','Someplace', 'NY', '12345', 1 )
```

If you inspect the auditlog, you'll see that the insertion was not logged because the trigger is defined for *UPDATEs*, not INSERTs. Change the author's last name with the following, however, and you'll see a log entry for the operation:

INPUT

```
UPDATE authors
SET au_lname = 'Carruthers'
WHERE au_id = '123-45-6789'
.
.
select * from auditlog
```

```
userName    operation   optime              object
..........  ..........  ..................  ..........,...
dbo         UPDATE      1999-05-23 19:09:00  authors

(1 row(s) affected)
```

So now you know what I was doing at seven o'clock on May 23, 1999! That's what auditing is for, I guess.

You could create a trigger to log inserts and deletes, too, or one that logged any or all three. A little later I'm going to show how to keep track of more detail like this.

Limitations of Triggers

Triggers are powerful constructs, but there are a few restrictions on the operations you can perform in a trigger. In general, no command that creates, alters, or drops any database object is allowed. I'd advise against these and any other time-consuming operation even if they were allowed, however. Your triggers should be as small as possible and only take those actions needed to get the job done.

You should also take into account *nesting* and *recursion*. Nesting refers to the possibility that the action taken by one trigger can cause another to execute. For example, if there were an insert trigger defined on the auditlog table, the auditing trigger's INSERT to the auditlog table would invoke the auditlog insert trigger. The second trigger would run to completion before the INSERT statement completed and the authors update trigger was resumed.

Recursion is when a piece of code, like a trigger, takes an action that causes it to be executed a second time from within the first invocation. In the example you've been looking at, this would occur if the hypothetical auditlog insert trigger updated a record on the authors table. When the update started, the update to authors would cause the update trigger to run again, inserting a record into the auditlog table, causing the insert trigger to update authors, and so on.

This would go on forever, but SQL Server has a global nesting/recursion limit of 32 levels. After that is exceeded, the original transaction that began the process is canceled and all changes within that transaction are rolled back. Recursive triggers have value in certain applications, but you should be wary of the kind of feedback loop I've described. If there's a possibility that it might occur, or that the number of recursions would exceed the limit, use a different mechanism.

Managing Triggers

Triggers are managed with the same sort of statements as are used for stored procedures. Instead of ALTER PROCEDURE and DROP PROCEDURE, of course, you use ALTER TRIGGER and DROP TRIGGER. You can inspect the text of the procedure with the sp_helptext procedure, or see what triggers are defined on a table with the stored procedure sp_helptrigger tableref[, type]. This procedure prints a list of the triggers defined for the table tableref, and you can optionally request only a particular type of trigger with the type parameter, which can be one of UPDATE, INSERT, or DELETE.

On the other hand, because the trigger's text is stored in the syscomments table, you can retrieve a quick listing of all the triggers in your database with the following SQL:

```
SELECT '

**** Trigger: ' + name + '

', text
FROM sysobjects
JOIN syscomments ON sysobjects.id = syscomments.id
WHERE type = 'TR'
```

This statement retrieves the text from syscomments for all the database objects in the current database that have a value of 'TR' for sysobjects.type, marking them as triggers.

Tip Retrieving information from sysobjects and syscomments is a useful feature when you are looking at a poorly documented database. (They do exist. Trust me.)

Special Tables: `Inserted` and `Deleted`

When your trigger is executed, there are two special tables that it can use to discover what is going on. `Inserted` and `deleted` contain the rows that are being inserted into the table or deleted from it, respectively. When an update occurs, it is reflected in these tables as deleting the old row values and inserting the new ones, so the `inserted` table contains the new row(s), and `deleted` contains the old value(s).

You can use these special tables to allow, reject, or take any other action appropriate based on the values the client submitted. You can modify unacceptable values to better ones (by changing the `inserted` table with UPDATE), record the data modifications to a log, or save deleted rows in an archive table (with the INSERT INTO...SELECT FROM syntax), or just about anything else you might want to do. Finally, you can reject a change altogether by canceling it with ROLLBACK TRANSACTION. Because the trigger executes in the context of the user query's transaction, rolling back from the trigger cancels *all* actions taken, not just changes to the table from which the trigger fired.

Listing 15.2 illustrates using these tables to log all insertions and deletions on the authors table.

LISTING 15.2   Auditing Data Values

```
CREATE TRIGGER author_insdel_audit
ON authors
FOR INSERT, DELETE
AS
    INSERT auditlog( userName, operation, optime, object )
        SELECT current_user, 'INSERTED', current_timestamp,
            au_id + ', ' + au_fname + ' ' + au_lname
        FROM inserted

    INSERT auditlog( userName, operation, optime, object )
        SELECT current_user, 'DELETED', current_timestamp,
            au_id + ', ' + au_fname + ' ' + au_lname
        FROM deleted
```

With the preceding trigger in place, the following SQL produces the output shown:

INPUT

```
DELETE authors
WHERE au_id = '123-45-6789'

INSERT authors
VALUES( '123-45-6789', 'Jones', 'Smith',
        '123 456-7890', '123 Main St.',
        'Someplace', 'NY', '12345', 1 )

SELECT * FROM auditlog
```

OUTPUT

```
userName   operation   optime                 object
--------   ---------   --------------------   ----------------
dbo        UPDATE      1999-05-23 19:09:00    authors
dbo        DELETED     1999-05-23 20:47:00    123-45-6789, ...
dbo        INSERiTED   1999-05-23 20:48:00    123-45-6789, ...
```

Experiment by modifying the update trigger to log changes by recording the old and new values for updates.

Take note that the preceding triggers are written so that they will execute correctly whether a change affects a single row or many. This is safest, but if performance is a problem, see the discussion in Books Online regarding multirow updates and triggers.

Summary

This lesson showed you the most capable mechanism in SQL Server, triggers, for controlling your data. You saw how to create triggers and work with them, and learned some issues to watch for when using them. The discussion ended with the special tables, inserted and deleted, which you can use to inspect the data changes being made.

In the next chapter, you're going to take a look at views, a logical construction you can use to simplify data for users, or control the data that they are able to see in a table.

LESSON 16

Simplifying Common Queries

This lesson teaches you a more sophisticated way of looking at your data and shows how you can simplify retrievals from your database.

Let's face it: The relational data model that you have been working with is powerful, but it isn't the simplest thing in the world to use. If there is anything that you need to do with structured information that you can't find a way to achieve with SQL, you just need to learn some more SQL. But that in no way implies that it's easy. In large databases with hundreds of tables, just figuring out which tables hold the pieces of individual entities is daunting. A single customer entity might be broken down and stored in twenty different tables or more, each recording a particular part of that customer's information.

A catalog describing all the objects in the database and their purpose, called a *data dictionary*, is indispensable for any but the most trivial of databases. A data dictionary only goes so far, though. In one fairly small project I was on, the data dictionary, diagrams, and subsection diagrams (drawings of smaller portions of the database in detail) showed more than 200 tables with thousands of columns in about 600 pages of design documents! Who but a full-time database administrator (DBA) is going to wade through that much hard-core technical mumbo jumbo to learn how to use the database? In fact, DBAs are usually so overworked that they might not have time, either. (Have you hugged your DBA today?)

The answer is clear: No one's interested in the database structure. Your users normally need access to the entities stored in the database, not the physical tables. You have to provide the data to users in a format that is useful to them, and 200 tables with thousands of relations, rules, and so forth won't meet their needs.

You know I'm going to propose a solution, don't you? The answer I suggest is a construct called a *view*. With a view, you can supply data objects from a query that pulls together meaningful information without requiring the user to know how to join all the tables in your database. You can also use views to restrict the data that users, for privacy or security reasons, are allowed to see.

 View   A *view*, which you'll learn more about later in the lesson, is a database object that you can use in a SELECT query as if it were a table. Instead of holding data itself, however, a view presents columns from a SQL query you provide. As you'll see, this can make it much easier to use data from your database.

Logical Versus Physical Data Model

I showed you the basic idea of logical and physical data models in Lesson 10, "An Interactive Web Application." When you design your database, you start from a set of business needs and from them develop a list of requirements for functions and data that your application will provide. There are more methodologies for building software than you can shake a stick at (even a very big stick), and even more for data modeling.

All methodologies that I've seen, however, have these two steps in common. First, define the data that you are going to store in the database in terms that are meaningful to the business. Then, break those business data items into database objects (tables, relations, constraints, procedures, triggers, and so forth) based on standard database design rules.

Why introduce the complexity of maintaining two different, but related, views of the data? The answer to this question has two aspects:

- *Flexibility*: When you separate fundamental pieces of logical items into separate tables, you have the ability to recombine them with SQL in different ways to meet different needs.

- *Efficiency*: The less data that is in a table, the quicker updates and retrievals will be because SQL Server has to work with less information. Designing your database to provide this efficiency takes care, but the potential return is large.

The flexibility side of the equation should be obvious. Efficiency could be harder to nail down, but not if you reflect on the discussion of retrieval performance in Lesson 11, "Improving Query Performance."

When you create your database, you are intentionally creating a storage structure that doesn't look like the objects that people in the business work with from day to day. You have to provide access to the data in a format that is meaningful to users who are familiar with the business, but don't care at all about the needs of a database designer. The view is a means to this end.

Views of Logical Objects

Views provide the mechanism to provide logical data items to users from the database. A view looks like a table to the user, containing information based on the data in the database. Unlike a table, you can define the view to combine, summarize, or partition data into a format that is appropriate to the user's needs, without modifying your physical design.

The SQL to create a view takes the following form:

```
CREATE VIEW viewname [( colname [, colname ...] )]
[ WITH ENCRYPTION ]
AS
     SELECTstmt
[WITH CHECK OPTION]
```

In this format, viewname is the name of the view, WITH ENCRYPTION functions as it does for triggers and stored procedure, and SELECTstmt is a query against the database. For an updateable view, WITH CHECK OPTION requires any update through the view to conform to the criteria in the SELECT the view is based on. That way, any rows added or changed through the view will still be visible through the view after the modification completes.

By default, the columns the view presents to the client will be named as they are in the SELECT on which the view is based. You can override the column names in the view definition with a replacement list of identifiers, the colname list in the syntax description. This can help keep the SELECT simple in the definition, but it can also be confusing if you have a large number of columns.

Views can be thought of as a cross between a table and a stored procedure. A view is defined as a named schema object that provides data from a query. Like a stored procedure, views are defined and stored in the database, but they cannot be parameterized like a procedure. Like a table, a view can be queried, but it cannot be updated unless it draws from one table only and all the columns that aren't exposed in the view are nullable or have default values.

Simplify

Create a view and you'll see what I mean. Consider the query used in Lesson 12 to retrieve authors' total sales from the authors, titleauthor, and titles tables:

```
SELECT au_fname+' '+ au_lname 'Author Name',
       SUM(ytd_sales * price) Sales
FROM authors
JOIN titleauthor ON authors.au_id = titleauthor.au_id
JOIN titles ON titleauthor.title_id = titles.title_id
GROUP BY authors.au_fname, authors.au_lname
```

This looks like information that is going to be useful in a number of different contexts, but do you want to force people to remember this query when they want to create a report from the data? For that matter, do you want to have to remember it? So use a view to store the query and present a pseudo-table called author_sales:

```
CREATE VIEW author_sales
AS
SELECT au_fname, au_lname, SUM(ytd_sales * price) sales
FROM authors
JOIN titleauthor ON authors.au_id = titleauthor.au_id
JOIN titles ON titleauthor.title_id = titles.title_id
GROUP BY authors.au_fname, authors.au_lname
```

Then issue queries against it as if it were just another table:

INPUT

```
SELECT *
FROM author_sales
WHERE sales > 150000
```

```
au_fname        au_lname                sales
- - - - - - - - -   - - - - - - - - - - - - - - - - - - - - - - -   - - - - - - - - - - - - - - - - - - - -
Reginald        Blotchet-Halls          180397.2000
Cheryl          Carson                  201501.0000
```

You can issue queries against the view to retrieve authors with a given sales level, as in the example, or to retrieve the sales value of a particular author, without knowing how what the underlying tables contain or how they are related to each other.

Partitioning Data

Another common use for views is *partitioning*, a term that in this context means breaking up data according to some defined rule. In some cases, you might only wish users to be able to see some of the columns in a table. For example, you could provide the example view of authors, but deny access to the authors table itself; users could use the view to retrieve sales information, but could not access private information like SSANs in the authors table itself. This form of partitioning is called *vertical* partitioning because it controls access to (vertical) columns.

Horizontal partitioning, on the other hand, scopes the data available by rows. In one application, I used horizontal partitioning to carve up a table containing tasking for members in a workgroup. In this case, the assigned team member was the criterion, so each person saw only those rows containing tasks that were assigned to them. In a larger database containing multiple departments' data in the same tables, you could make the database more usable by filtering out other departments' data from what you showed to a user.

Figure 16.1 shows a comparison between vertical and horizontal partitioning; view vwVertical shows columns from the table, whereas vwHorizontal shows only selected rows. Vertical partitioning, as I mentioned, involves only selecting those columns the user should see into the view. Horizontal partitioning is accomplished by using the WHERE clause to limit the rows returned.

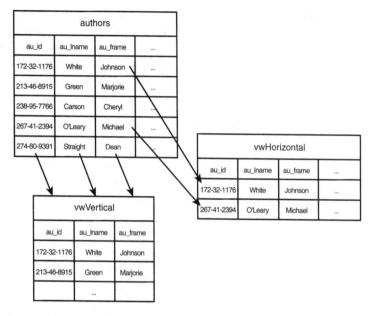

FIGURE 16.1   Partitioning data.

Problems with Views

One drawback to views is performance. SQL Server will optimize the query plan to a point, but it has to follow the rules: Underneath the view, the view's SQL still must be planned and executed with each query on the view.

Consider the following query against the author_sales view, which joins back to the authors table to get the author id:

```
SELECT  author_sales.au_fname, author_sales.au_lname,
        au_id, sales
FROM author_sales
JOIN authors ON authors.au_fname = author_sales.au_fname
            AND authors.au_lname = author_sales.au_lname
```

If you look at the query plan for this retrieval in Query Analyzer, you will see a large query tree executing the SQL on which the view is based, and an additional index scan to retrieve the author id based on the JOIN in the query. The SQL to retrieve the data directly is better optimized, and so is about 10% faster. On the other hand, it requires direct knowledge of the tables and their relations to construct:

```
SELECT au_fname, au_lname, authors.au_id au_id,
       SUM(ytd_sales * price) sales
FROM authors
JOIN titleauthor ON authors.au_id = titleauthor.au_id
JOIN titles ON titleauthor.title_id = titles.title_id
GROUP BY authors.au_id, authors.au_fname, authors.au_lname
```

Your performance results will vary. What won't is the flexibility views give you in cutting down the work of retrieving data. You should apply this mechanism when it is appropriate, and you might need to strike a balance between the usability you gain and the cost in performance.

The other drawback you might or might not encounter is complexity, but if it's an issue, you will probably find it's a "pay me now or pay me later" situation. The project I mentioned earlier used a table structure that was, for the most part, well distributed in terms of breaking logical entities into physical tables, so inserts and updates could be carried out with a high degree of concurrency. With the data spread out, on any given update to the database, the chance of one user conflicting with another was minimized, so the database design would scale well.

However, the code that retrieved logical entities from that database was the most complicated SQL I have ever seen. Views were constructed to synthesize entities from sometimes only loosely related data. In this case, putting those business objects together required at least one query containing more than 2,000 lines of SQL. Can you imagine what it would have been like if the application had to code that sort of query everywhere it was used? The views were complicated, but without them the application would have been much more difficult.

Summary

In this lesson I've described some of the issues in providing a business-meaningful representation of the data in your database, and presented the view as a mechanism to handle the problem. Whenever you build a database, you will have to balance technology issues of the database's physical structure against the accessibility of the data to users who aren't necessarily SQL gurus like you. The view is a schema object that directly addresses that problem by helping you bring the data together in a form that is more meaningful to other users of the database.

That's all I'm going to teach you about database construction with SQL Server. Next, you're going to look at SQL Enterprise Manager and some of the features it has to make working with databases easier. Later lessons will introduce you to concepts in security, backups, and data migration.

LESSON 17

Managing Databases the Easy Way

In this lesson, you'll see how to use SQL Server Enterprise Manager to work with servers, databases, and database objects.

Constructing and managing a database can be a time-consuming task, so the better the tools, the happier I am. SQL Server 7's management interface, SQL Server Enterprise Manager, is much better than it was in version 6.5, and the older one wasn't bad to start with! There are going to be some things that you can do with Enterprise Manager, like working with databases, that you have already gone through doing in SQL. Before you ask the obvious question, I'll ask it for you: If you can do it in the GUI, why bother with the SQL? There are two reasons:

- Enterprise Manager is a management tool for maintaining servers. Though there are some features that are useful to the rest of us, it's really most useful to administrators.

- When you build a solution based on a database, the database objects your application uses are just as important a part of the application as the client you create is. You should keep a copy of the SQL to create and initialize your database in the same place you keep your forms, scripts, and so forth. This makes it easier to distribute copies of your application to others, to set up independent development environments, and to document your application, among other things.

- Many tasks for constructing and maintaining databases are easier and more efficiently performed with SQL.

This lesson is going to introduce you to Enterprise Manager and give you a quick run through of where to find things.

Working in SQL Server Enterprise Manager

The Enterprise Manager interface is shown in Figure 17.1. Enterprise manager is a snap-in object in Microsoft's Management Console (MMC), so it can coexist with other MMC-based management tools like the Exchange and IIS management interfaces.

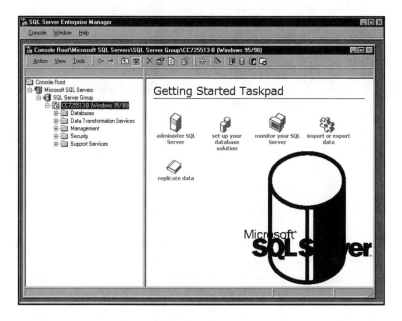

FIGURE 17.1   SQL Server Enterprise Manager.

Enterprise Manager, like other MMC applications, presents a tree presentation of the databases you work with. In the tree view, the first node under Microsoft SQL Servers is the SQL Server Group, an object created by the setup program when the software is installed. You can create additional groups of servers to organize your view of servers on your network. By default, the local server is added to SQL Server Group, but you can *register* additional servers by right-clicking the group and selecting New SQL Server Registration... from the pop-up menu.

When you're working with Enterprise Manager, you can either manipulate the objects you want to work with directly from the tree view, or you can use the "task pad" interface you see in the right view when you click on the server name.

Under a database server in the tree, you will see the folders listed in Table 17.1.

Table 17.1   Nodes in the Server Subtree

Node	Contents
Databases	Databases, of course
Data Transformation Services	Information for repeated data transfers and data warehousing
Management	Logs, scheduled tasking, backup, and monitoring information
Security	Logins, roles, and server registration
Support Services	Distributed transaction and mail integration

As usual, anything with a plus-box next to it can be expanded to show subelements. You can work with many items by either left-clicking and choosing a task from the taskpad page that appears in the right pane, or by right-clicking and selecting a function from the context menu. Context menus usually have a subset of available operations, and an `All tasks` submenu that provides more options.

The parts of the tree that are available to you can vary depending on your roles and permissions in the database. I'll discuss some that I think might be useful to you, but you might not be able to use all features I mention.

`SQL Server Agent`, under the `Management` node, is your interface to the task scheduler I mentioned to you in Lesson 1, "What Is SQL Server?" This service runs jobs for you at scheduled times for maintenance, replication, warehousing, and so forth. You can also define *alerts* based on SQL Server error notifications, and *operators* that SQL Server will email or page when those alert conditions are met.

The `Current Activity` node shows what's going on in your database. You can choose to view the processes in the system, the locks held by processes, or the locks held on objects.

Tip   Unfortunately, the tabular view of locks that was in the Enterprise Manager of version 6.5 seems to have been lost in version 7. You can get a lot better view using the system stored procedure sp_lock in Query Analyzer. For more on this and other monitoring functions, look at "Monitoring Server Performance and Activity" under the Administering SQL Server book in Books Online.

When you have strange things happening or reliability problems with your server, take a look at the SQL Server logs. These log files record information about processing errors in the database server software, networking errors, and device problems, like bad data in a disk file. These logs are *aged off* by numbering. When SQL Server starts, the sixth archive disappears, the fifth becomes the sixth, and so on up to the current log from the previous session, which becomes archive number one, and then SQL Server begins a new current log file.

You can also manage additional services that are installed on your computer, or use the Security tab to manage user roles, logins, and server connections for distributed server installations. I'll discuss security more in the next lesson, but I won't be able to get into multi-server applications; that would take a book of its own.

Creating Databases

To create a database, you can use either the task pad interface or the Databases context menu, on the server where the database should be.

To use the task pad interface, click on the server you are going to put the database on, and click the Set up your database solution on the tasks pane. On the resulting page, shown in Figure 17.2, you can perform a number of common tasks in SQL Server, including creating databases and database objects, or jump to Query Analyzer or Books Online.

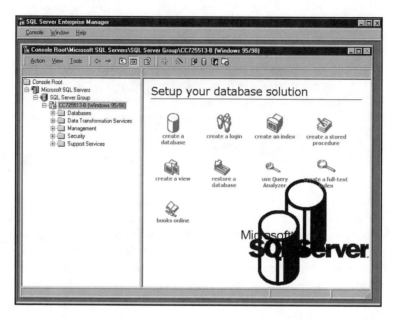

Figure 17.2 The Database Solution Page in SQL Enterprise Manager.

If you click the Create database icon, you'll see the Create Database Wizard. This wizard leads you through naming the database, specifying the locations for files to hold the data and transaction log, and then lists for you the options you have chosen so you can confirm them before it creates the database.

Creating a database from the Databases node's context menu is no more difficult to use, and is quicker to access, than the wizard. You can also set database options before you create the database, which the wizard does not allow. If you right-click the Databases node and click New database... on the context menu, you see the dialog box shown in Figure 17.3.

On the General tab, name your database, and then set up the files your database will use. To specify a file, click in the column under each title in the Database files grid in the middle of the dialog box. A text input box appears into which you can enter the information for that column. The first file in the list will be in the PRIMARY file group, but you can specify the file group for any additional files you add. Size and growth settings for each file are defined by clicking the file in the grid, and then adjusting the properties for that file at the bottom of the page. The Transaction Log page sets the same properties for the transaction log files.

FIGURE 17.3 Database Properties dialog box—General tab.

The Options page allows you to set database options on the database when it is created. Each option includes a short description underneath of what it is. Some commonly used options are described in Table 17.2.

TABLE 17.2 Commonly Used Database Options

Option	Use
DBO use only	Keeps users other than the owner out of the database; good for maintenance and setup. This is a nice option because users currently logged in can finish what they are doing, but when logged out, cannot log back in if they aren't the owner.
Single user	Allows only one user to use the database at a time; required if you want to rename the database or restore from a backup.
Recursive triggers	Enables recursive trigger firing as described in Lesson 15, "Controlling How Changes Are Made."
Truncate log on checkpoint	Truncates log entries every time a checkpoint completes. *Use with caution.*

Truncate log on checkpoint requires a little explanation. The log referred to is the transaction log. During database operation, the transaction log collects a large number of transactions because every operation is usually recorded there. Eventually it can fill up, or if you've allowed it to grow automatically, it can become very large. You'll normally truncate (empty out) the transaction log when you back up the database, freeing space for new transactions.

If you turn the truncate on checkpoint option on, though, SQL Server will automatically truncate at each checkpoint it completes. In normal operation, SQL Server does not immediately write data you modify to disk; instead, it queues up, writes, and then sends them to the disk periodically, speeding up response time to queries. The process of reconciling the disk data files with data waiting in memory is called a *checkpoint*. After a checkpoint, the data on disk is assured to be up to date and consistent, so the transactions recorded before the checkpoint are no longer needed to recover the server if it crashes or the power goes out. The truncate on checkpoint option tells SQL Server to clean up the old transactions after it completes each checkpoint.

Though this keeps the transaction log size down and everything tidy, there are definite problems with it:

- Those old transactions are there to recover your database from the last backup if the data files get trashed, so if you set this option, you won't be able to recover any updates since you backed up—all the transactions since then will be erased.

- In high-volume environments, where the database is constantly being updated, the truncation process can impact performance.

- This option cannot be used if you are replicating databases.

If you know and accept the risks and limitations involved, this setting can be useful; your priorities for data security and your backup plan will determine if this option is appropriate for you.

I've detailed some of the options on the Database Properties dialog because you will see the same dialog if you return to modify an existing database. With the knowledge you've already gained, most of the elements you'll see will be familiar to you already.

Creating Database Objects

Underneath each database node in Enterprise Manager are nodes containing the database objects that exist in the database: tables, views, stored procedures, and so forth. This is one of the nicest parts of Enterprise Manager because for most objects, you can double-click to edit the properties of the object. Creating objects is as easy as right-clicking the node representing the kind of object you want, and then clicking New *object-type*. For example, if you create a new table in this manner, you see the New Table display, as in Figure 17.4.

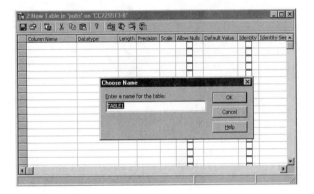

FIGURE 17.4   New Table spreadsheet.

After you enter a name for the new table, you can type in column names, types, sizes, and so forth in the spreadsheet provided. To see the same display for an existing table, you have to click Design table... on its context menu. For all objects, modifications are subject to the same restrictions as when you change them with the ALTER statement. When you click the disk icon to save, the changes are written to the database and the new table is created (or the existing one modified).

A very nice feature of version 7.0 is the Diagrams node, illustrated in Figure 17.5. Under this node you can create a diagram showing all or some subset of the tables and relations in your database. This is not a hugely useful tool for database design because it does not store the schema in an independent file; when you make a change to a database element, the database structure is immediately modified to reflect the changes. Though this can be useful in small projects, it doesn't work well for more complicated efforts. However, for exploring databases or creating online references for a database you work with, it's one of those tools that, after using it, you don't want to be without.

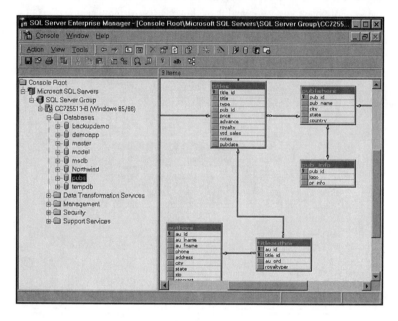

FIGURE 17.5   A Database Diagram in SQL Server Enterprise Manager.

Scripting Database Objects

I've emphasized the importance of maintaining the SQL to create your database outside the database itself. Enterprise Manager provides some enticing interfaces for creating databases and database objects without using SQL, though. It would be a shame if there was no way to reconcile the two. But SQL Server provides a facility to generate SQL scripts from a database so you can use the GUI to create items, and then generate SQL you can distribute or maintain elsewhere.

If you choose **Generate SQL Scripts...** from the **All tasks** submenu on a database's context menu, you will see the Generate SQL Scripts dialog box. On the General tab shown, you can select the database objects that will be scripted, and the Formatting tab lets you specify detail information about how to lay out the script.

The Options tab provides some more important selections. Here you can choose to include user logins, roles, and permissions in the security section; to script "peripheral" objects like indices, triggers, and keys in the table section; and specify what sort of files to create in the file section. Whenever you script your database, you should move to this tab and turn on all the extra database items you have created in your database; I don't know why they are turned off by default (particularly the primary key, index, and triggers options) because these items will often be critical to your database.

When you have set the options as you wish and click **OK**, you'll have the opportunity to specify a file or location in which to store the resultant files, and then the database will crunch for a while creating SQL scripts that will recreate it.

You should be careful of two things in this process: the database itself and user logins. Creating the database itself will not be scripted; you will have to add that to the resulting script if you want the database to be created in a fully automatic operation. In addition, the statements to create users are scripted with no password. Because the users' passwords are stored in hashed form, their passwords cannot be retrieved to include in the script (nor would you want them to be). You must either manually edit the SQL to provide default passwords, or edit the users in Enterprise Manager in whatever new databases you create with the script. Otherwise, anyone will be able to log in as anyone else, because no one will have a password.

With the scripting feature, you can create a database, tables, users, and any other database objects that must be in the database, and then generate the SQL to recreate them on another database or another server. Though you should not do this on a large project, for small efforts, this can be a quick and efficient method to build the database without giving up the capability to recreate it from scratch.

Summary

SQL Enterprise Manager is full of features that make it easier to manage databases, but not all of them will necessarily be useful to everyone. In this lesson, I've shown you some common tasks and methods for using Enterprise Manager to work with your database, and some details on items you will probably use. I finished by showing you how to export your database structure by generating SQL from it in Enterprise Manager. Next, you're going to look at two sides of keeping your data safe: backing it up and controlling access to it.

LESSON 18
Keeping Your Server Safe

This lesson teaches you how to keep your database safe by backing it up and controlling access to it.

This lesson is going to show you some features SQL Server provides to help keep your data secure from disasters and from unauthorized access. You should design your security and backup strategies as carefully as the database itself if your data are of any value to you.

Backing Up Your Database

SQL Server's backup copies your data to *backup devices*, which can be conventional backup media such as a tape drive or disk files you can back up with external tools or store on a safe repository elsewhere. When you create the backup, the file or tape(s) the backup occupies is the *backup set*.

There are several kinds of backups you can do; you don't have to back up the entire database each time:

- *Full backup*: A full backup, one that copies the entire database, must be done at least once.

- *Differential backup*: After you perform the first full backup, you can choose a differential backup to save only the rows that have changed since the last full backup.

- *Transaction log backup*: In lieu of a differential backup, you can perform a transaction log backup, which saves all the transactions since the last time the transaction log was backed up.

- *File or filegroup backups*: You can also create file or filegroup backups, but in most cases a database backup is more useful for the same needs.

On smaller databases, you may elect to perform a full backup every time, but with a larger database this can waste both time and backup media. You'll typically plan your backups to include occasional full backups, with frequent differential or transaction log backups in between.

Backup Strategies

When you form your database backup strategy, you should establish a schedule that specifies the frequency and type of backups you will perform. When designing the backup plan, you should first decide what it is you need to get from the backups in the event of a failure, and then create your backup plan to secure the data in accordance with those needs. Finally, plan out ahead of time what needs to be done to recover from failures in a written recovery plan. Even if the database is your own personal setup, used by no one else, you'll feel better when something goes wrong if you know in advance how to recover.

Tip   Regardless of the form and size of your database, if there is business-critical data in it, *please* include off-site storage of periodic backups! Fires, earthquakes, and floods happen, but disasters are not limited to those of the natural kind. A local Internet service provider was taken off line one night last year when someone broke into the building that housed its servers and made off with the equipment! Though such occurrences are rare, I assume that the eventuality you fail to plan for is the one that will occur.

There are four things to safeguard in your backup plan:

- Your previous backups
- Your system databases
- Your user databases
- Your transaction logs

Except for the case in which you back up the entire database every time you back up, restoring it will require at least a full backup set and one or more differential or transaction log backup sets. Because data can be corrupted and the error not detected until much later, your backup plan should address storage and retention of previous backups.

The system databases, `master` and `msdb`, store system-wide information on user logins, databases, devices, jobs, operators, and so forth. Although it's difficult to ensure that the database is backed up on the schedule Microsoft suggests, you should back up the system databases regularly. (Microsoft suggests you back it up each time `master` is changed, for example, but each time a user changes their password, `master` is changed!) If you add your own objects to `model`, it needs to be backed up, too.

You need to look to specific failure scenarios in planning for recovery. The database data and transaction log are the focus of your backup plan, of course; the degree of surety you need in their preservation is the main variable in your backup planning. You should specify what failures you're addressing, how much and how recent the data you will be able to recover is, and how long the database might be off line while you recover. Users, management, or anyone else who has a stake in the database should sign off on these specifics before you implement the plan.

Backing Up

You can back up interactively or schedule the backups to happen periodically without user intervention. Interactively, you might either use Enterprise Manager or the BACKUP command in Query Analyzer. Because you will usually either schedule the backup or use Enterprise Manager, those are the methods I will discuss here. For information on the BACKUP command, please see SQL Server's Books Online.

Regardless of the method of backup, you usually create a backup device first. The device can be a disk file on the local computer or a network share, or a tape drive that is installed and configured on the server; you can back up to a network-connected disk, but you cannot back up to a tape on another computer without additional software.

Tip Disk backups don't have to have a preexisting device; you can back up directly to a file. It's generally easier to manage backups, though, if you set up the device.

To create a backup device, go to the Management node in Enterprise manager. Right-click the Backup node and choose New Backup Device... from the context menu to display the Backup Device Properties dialog box, as in Figure 18.1. Give the device a name, and then enter the name of the file or tape to which the backup data will go; for tapes, the device name should be the physical device name (for example, \\.\tape0). For disk files, either give the drive and path for the file on the local computer, or use the UNC file path to a remote file, in the form *servername**sharename**path**filename*, where *servername* is the name of the server, *sharename* is the disk share on that computer, and *path* and *filename* specify the file on that share.

Figure 18.1   Creating a new backup device.

Tip Disk backups are a handy, low-cost method for backups in a small network. If you have a file server with an existing backup process, you can back up your database to files on the file server and have them picked up in the existing plan. If you choose this approach, you'll need to coordinate backup schedules; because file backup tools usually won't back up files that are open when the backup is run, you need to make sure your database backup isn't running when the file server's backup executes.

After you've set up your devices, you can back up a database by choosing
All tasks, Backup Database... from the database's context menu, or by
clicking backup database under the Backup section in the task pad page
for the database. Either method displays the SQL Server Backup window
shown in Figure 18.2.

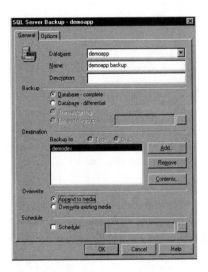

FIGURE 18.2   Starting a backup.

The name and the description you specify for the backup will be shown
when you view the contents of a backup later. The backup type selects
the types I've discussed, and the destination is the device or file where the
backup will go. You can choose to append information (add it to the backup
media, preserving existing backups there) or overwrite any existing data. If
you choose the Schedule button and then click the ellipsis button (...), you
can set a one-time or recurring backup schedule. This *very* useful feature
will set up a SQL Server Agent job for you that runs the SQL BACKUP command on the schedule you specify. You can view or edit this job in the Jobs
node of SQL Server Agent's area of the Management subtree.

The Options tab lets you set other options for the backup. Verify backup
upon completion will reread the data and make sure it got to the device
correctly. Remove inactive entries from transaction log, available
only on a transaction log backup, will truncate old entries from the log
after they are backed up. The initialization option enables you to clear out

and assign a name to the media (tape or disk file) the backup is going to. If you assign a name and expiration date to the media (using the Backup set will expire option), SQL Server can read the name and expiration date on the backup set and keep you from accidentally overwriting a recent backup.

After you've backed up your data, see that the media is safely controlled according to your backup plan.

Restoring

Restoring a database requires different activities depending on what it is that you want to restore and why. Usually the problem will be that your data got destroyed by errant SQL, or your server has failed for some reason. It is a little risky to restore a database whose data files just plain got destroyed, but it is possible if the transaction log survived.

The first thing to do if your database gets trashed is to back up everything, including the transaction log. If you can't back up through Enterprise Manager, as will be the case if you lost the data files, copy the transaction log and data files to another server or back them up with normal file backup software. You should stop SQL Server while you're doing this. The Restore database window is shown in Figure 18.3.

Figure 18.3   Restoring a database.

The General tab enables you to restore a database or individual files, or to select a backup set from a device to restore a specific database backup from the sets on a tape or file device. SQL Server maintains a history of the backups you've done on databases, so it's easy to select a backup or series of backups from the Database backup display. If you're rebuilding a server after a crash, you might need to use the From device option and restore the data into a new database.

If you only want to restore to a certain point in time, you can do that by setting the time to restore the database to. Use this option if a user scrammed the database with an ill-advised delete. When you click OK and the restore executes, SQL Server will recreate the database as it was at the time you specified.

After you've picked the backup(s) to restore, you can change to the Options tab to set restore behaviors. Most of these options are self-explanatory, except Recovery completion state. To restore the database to where it was before a failure, you need to restore the last full backup, and then any differential or transaction log backups since. It's easiest if all the backups are on one file or tape, but if not, you'll have to restore the last full backup, and then each transaction log since in order. Set one of the "Leave database non-operational..." choices under Recovery Completion state for all but the last restore. When you restore the most recent log, set the Leave database operational... choice.

There is one more step you can take after restoring from backup to recover right to the point of failure. This step will only work correctly if you were able to restore the last full backup and *all* log backups since then, and you saved off the file(s) holding the log that was in use since the last log backup. If these conditions are all true, detach the database or shut down SQL Server (the latter is easiest) and restore the log files that you saved to their original location. When you restart SQL Server, SQL Server will roll forward (reapply) the transactions that were committed before the failure occurred, restoring the database state right to the time of failure.

Any time you restore the database, you will be overwriting large amounts of data in it. Therefore, your first step in recovery should be to back up your database's current state so you can back out any changes you make in recovery. After that, your actions depend on what broke and what you want to get back. There is a lot more information available in the SQL Server Books Online regarding backup strategies and operations, and though this lesson will get you started, I strongly advise you to at least glance through the books so you know what information is there.

Controlling Access

No backup strategy will un-compromise your data. You can recover from data destruction, but when unauthorized users access your data (for example, posting your credit card billing history to the Internet), you can never un-lose that information. SQL Server controls database access based on *logins*, *roles*, and *permissions*.

Each user is identified by a *login* when they access the server. This can either be a login maintained by SQL Server, or a Windows NT domain login maintained by NT. The server login allows a user to establish a session with the server, but doesn't immediately provide access to any databases.

User *roles* are categories in which you can group people to control access. There are several predefined *server* roles in SQL Server you can use, but you can neither add nor delete from the list. You can define additional roles for user groups or business divisions like Accounting or Human Resources in individual databases. By controlling access according to roles where possible, you can simplify security procedures.

Permissions are where all this is going. For every database object, you can *grant* or *deny* the capability to perform operations on those objects to user logins or roles. By requiring users to be identified and then controlling their actions based on the permissions granted to them, you can provide information and features to only the users who need them.

Server Logins and Roles

To allow a user to log in to the server, an administrator can create a SQL Server login for the user or grant the capability to log in to an NT user or the members of an NT group. You create a login with the sp_addlogin system stored procedure; this procedure performs a number of checks on the login you're creating (you can see its operation by looking at the procedure with sp_helptext), and then adds the user to the server security tables. The procedure has a number of parameters, but the most commonly used are the first three:

- The name of the login to create
- The password for the new login

The default database for the user

The last item is the database in which the user will start out when he logs in.

 Caution   When SQL Server is installed, the sa user has no password. Don't leave it that way.

If you want to allow an NT user into the database, you use the sp_grantlogin procedure instead. This procedure takes only one parameter, the user or group's Windows NT identifier in the form *domain_name\user_or_group_name*.

After the login is created, you can assign the user to server roles. These are listed in Table 18.1.

TABLE 18.1   Predefined Server Roles

Role	Capability
dbcreator	Adds or modifies databases
diskadmin	Adds, modifies, or removes devices
processadmin	Kills processes
securityadmin	Manipulates logins and permissions
serveradmin the server	Changes server configuration and shuts down
setupadmin	Manages linked servers and startup procedures
sysadmin	sysadmin does anything sysadmin wants

These roles are system-wide capabilities and are concerned with *granting* a user permission to do things, not with restricting their action. If you are

administering a SQL Server, you can add users to these roles to allow
them to perform maintenance tasks; you might, for example, grant help
desk operators the securityadmin and processadmin roles so they could
maintain users and kill runaway processes.

Security on Databases

Within a database, you have much finer control over users and roles than
you do at the server level. When you create a database, no users (except
the system administrators and the user who created the database, hereafter
known as the database owner, or *dbo*) have access to the database or
anything in it. After creating the database, you can grant users access to
the database by adding their logins to the database and grant them access
to the objects in the database using the GRANT statement. Finally, you can
create database roles, grant or deny permissions to the roles, and then add
users to the roles to apply those permissions to the users.

> **Note** I'm going to show you how to accomplish
> these tasks using SQL because it is generally faster
> than using SQL Server Enterprise Manager. If you pre-
> fer, you can use the permissions page in many objects'
> Properties dialog to control access to the object.

You add a login to the database with the sp_grantdbaccess stored procedure. This allows the user with that login to change context to the database
with the USE *dbname* statement. It does not, however, provide them access to
the objects in the database. You must either grant them access to individual
objects, or assign them a role that has the access you require them to have.

Here again, SQL Server provides predefined roles for you to use. You can
create new roles in the database, though, and assign the new roles permissions you determine. The predefined roles are described in Table 18.2.

TABLE 18.2   Predefined Database Roles

Role	Capability
db_accessadmin	Adds or removes users
db_backupoperator	Backs up the database

Role	Capability
db_datareader	Reads data in any user tables
db_datawriter	Inserts and updates user tables
db_ddladmin	Adds, alters, or drops objects
db_denydatareader	Can't read anything
db_denydatawriter	Can't write anything
db_owner	The owner of the database (dbo)
db_securityadmin	Modifies roles and role members; sets permissions on database objects

With the server, there is a single user with the authority to do anything (the sa user); within the database, the database owner, dbo, has similar control over the database.

You use sp_addrole *role* [, *ownername*] to add a role to the database, where *role* is the name for the role. You can specify a different user as the owner with *ownername* if you want to allow a different user to administer the role.

After a role is created, you use the stored procedure sp_addrolemember *role, user* to add a user to the role, where *role* is the name of the role, and *user* is the name of the database user (or another role) you are assigning that role. Thereafter, whatever permissions you have granted or denied that role will be applied to the user or role you added, too.

Permissions

When any object is created, from a database on down, the object is owned by the creator, who has complete control over it. The creator grants or revokes permissions to other users on the object, or can deny permissions to a user or role that would otherwise have that permission.

As a system administrator, you can grant or deny permission to execute certain statements with GRANT *statement* TO *user*. The statements you can grant in this manner include the CREATE statements for schema objects (for example, CREATE DATABASE or CREATE TABLE), or the BACKUP DATABASE and

BACKUP LOG statements. You can include multiple statements separated by
commas to grant multiple permissions in one step.

Use the statement GRANT permission ON object TO user_or_role in
a database to give permission related to an object to a user or role. The
permission you can grant depends on the object you're referring to,
and it's only appropriate to some objects, but in general they are what
you would expect. The permissions you can grant on objects are shown
in Table 18.3.

TABLE 18.3   Object Permissions

Objects	Available Permissions
Stored procedure or extended stored procedure	EXECUTE
Table, view, column	DML: SELECT, INSERT, UPDATE and DELETE, plus REFERENCES.

The only unusual one in the lot is the REFERENCES permission: Because a
table that is the target of another table's foreign key cannot be dropped, it
places constraints on what you can do with that table if another table references it. You can therefore control the ability to place that constraint on
your table.

REVOKE and DENY use the same syntax as GRANT. REVOKE takes away a
permission that was previously granted to a user or role, but does nothing
else if, for example, a user didn't have that permission in the first place.
DENY is more imperative; it denies a permission, whether the user has it
or not, no matter how the user gained it. A DENY takes precedence over
any GRANT.

As an example, imagine you have a role *Hill* with the members *Jack* and
Jill. If you grant SELECT access to a table to the role *Hill*, both *Jack* and *Jill*
can retrieve data from the table. Using REVOKE to keep *Jack* out of the table
(with REVOKE SELECT ON tablename TO jack) will not be effective; as a
member of *Hill*, he will still have access. To keep *Jack* out, you have to use
DENY SELECT ON tablename TO jack.

Summary

This lesson covered backing up and restoring databases, and the basics of security controls in SQL Server. Your backup and security plans are the main tools you have in SQL Server to keep your data safe from mistakes, disasters, disgruntled employees, and for that matter, buggy code. Smaller databases with fewer users will need mainly to focus on maintaining good backups, but as the user pool and the database get larger, or if you include private or financial information, you need to start thinking about security and controlling access to information that shouldn't be spread around.

LESSON 19

Monitoring Activity

In this lesson, you'll learn how to monitor activity in your database and save a record of activity for analysis or replay.

You'll often find that your database work doesn't produce the results you wanted right out of the box. The results can range anywhere from odd, like lost updates or poor performance, to causing an application you've created to crash; but regardless, you will need to find out what happened. High-level tools like Access or middleware like ASP don't always make it obvious what went wrong, so a tool that lets you see the SQL that is sent to the database is invaluable.

Just such a tool is SQL Profiler. Similar to the SQL Trace program included in SQL Server 6.x, Profiler lets you register servers and then define and execute traces that collect events that occur in the database. With Profiler, you get a low-level view of all or a part of the activity in your database, a valuable aid in debugging and tuning your analytic work or application development.

Creating Traces

In Profiler, you work with a *trace*, a snapshot of database activity that you capture during the database's operation. In a trace, you record all the events that match criteria you specify so that you can analyze activity, debug applications, or replay the events you captured to evaluate changes you make.

 Caution Be careful when monitoring activity to gauge performance. Try to capture only the events you need without overly limiting your data acquisition. Tracing requires server resources and can conflict with your application, so the more you trace, the more you risk skewing your results.

Start SQL Profiler by selecting Profiler from your Microsoft SQL Server 7.0 menu. When the program starts, you can register a server, create a trace, or start a trace collecting data. If you have run traces and saved them, you can reload the events you captured and replay them against the server, as well. I'll look at all of these operations.

If you haven't registered the server you want to monitor yet, you'll need to choose Register SQL Server from the Tools menu. This is similar to the process you use in SQL Enterprise Manager to register a server, and just informs Profiler of the existence of the SQL Servers on your network. When you've registered a server, you can create and execute a trace of the activity on that server.

Defining a Trace

You create a trace with the File, New, Trace option on the main menu of the Profiler window. This produces the Trace Properties dialog shown in Figure 19.1.

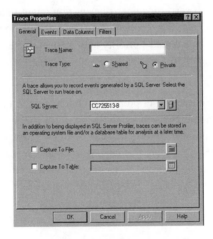

FIGURE 19.1 Trace Properties in SQL Server Profiler.

The four tabs in the Properties dialog box let you set general options, identify the information you need to monitor, and set filters on the captured data.

On the General tab, perform the following steps:

1. Give the trace a name.

2. Select either Shared to enable other users logging in to your computer to use the trace definition, or Private to keep the definition in your own profile only.

3. Specify the server to monitor.

4. Select a file or table to capture into if you want to keep a record of your trace.

 Tip   If you don't tell the program to record the captures here, you can still use the Save option on the File menu to save data from a capture after collecting it.

The trace is collected by a trace thread and deposited into a queue for return to Profiler. If server loading is heavy, you might find that the queue fills before it can be sent to Profiler and events start getting lost. You can modify both the trace thread's priority and the queue size to stop this from happening, at the risk of interfering with normal operations and gathering inaccurate results.

If you click the Source Server properties button (next to the server drop-down on the General tab), you see the window shown in Figure 19.2. This window sets the number of rows that can be in the queue on the server, how long an object that should be logged will wait for space if the log queue fills up, and the priority changes for the collection thread.

FIGURE 19.2   Source Server properties.

You can limit the information gathered in a trace on the Events tab. Under Available events are all monitored events in SQL Server; as you add events to the Selected events box, they disappear from the available list.

 Caution   If you plan to save the captured data for later analysis, choose your events carefully, as only the events you capture will be available for use later.

The Data Columns tab is similar to the Events tab, except whereas Events defines what occurrences you'll record, the columns you capture are the types of information you'll record about those occurrences. You can capture the statements, process identifiers, user IDs, and any part of a raft of other information. It might take a bit of experimentation to find exactly the information profile you need—the good news is that, with the broad selection available, you'll probably be able to find what you want.

The Filters tab lets you include or exclude events by criteria you specify. You can filter by process ID, user ID, CPU usage, or whatever is appropriate to your analysis. In general, you select a criterion type (like CPU), and then fill in the information in the blanks at the bottom of the dialog that the filter needs. This information will vary on the type of filter criterion; with the CPU filter, you can provide a minimum or maximum value, whereas with the Application Name filter you can supply an application name that Profiler will monitor or ignore.

 Tip   Unless the volume of activity on your server requires some initial filtering, I'd leave them alone until you've captured some information and can see how it should be tailored.

When you click **OK** to create the trace, it's saved using the name you gave it so you can retrieve the definition later. Because the trace definitions are stored in the Registry, you can't delete them as you would a file in a directory. Use the Delete Traces option on the File menu to get rid of definitions you don't need any more.

Running a Trace

When you create a trace definition, by default you drop into it immediately. You can also run a trace by clicking the play icon on the main toolbar; this invokes a dialog box listing the traces that you have defined. Select one from the list and click **OK** to start the trace.

Figure 19.3 shows a trace window as it's collecting information. Trace windows are "live" displays because they show you the activity on your server as it occurs. As the information scrolls upward, you will often want to see events that have gone by already. Use the far-right button on the trace window's toolbar to turn off the "auto-scroll" behavior first, or the window will jump back to the end every time an event occurs.

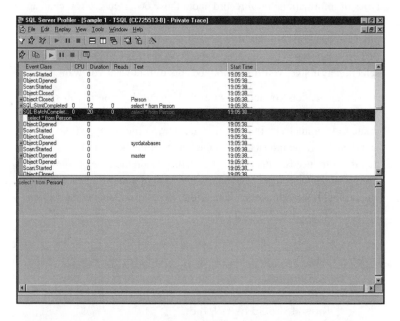

FIGURE 19.3 A Profiler Trace window.

To simplify trace creation, Profiler includes the Create Trace Wizard on the Tools menu, illustrated in Figure 19.4. With the wizard, you can use predefined query profiles to address specific problems, target one database or the whole server, and limit your collection to one application or all applications using the server.

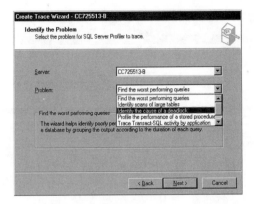

FIGURE 19.4 The Create Trace Wizard.

Saving and Replaying Captures

When you've collected data you feel will be useful for analysis, you can save it to a file or table; if you specified where to save the data in the trace definition, it's saved automatically. You can still, however, save the data from the current session to a table or file other than the one(s) specified in the trace definition.

If you open a saved trace file or table, you'll see a window similar to that in Figure 19.5. The trace file window shows events in the top half and explanatory text in the bottom, like the trace windows, but instead of having the tape-player style control buttons, these windows have Visual Studio-type debugging buttons on them. Use these buttons to start, pause, single-step, or stop replaying events that were captured in the saved trace.

You can use a trace window to look back over an event trace, but its real value is in being able to replay events to gauge the effects of changes you've made. When you replay a trace, Profiler will send the same SQL to the server that you or your application did in the session you recorded originally. If, for example, you are trying to improve performance, you can play back the same trace against the database over and over as you try different approaches.

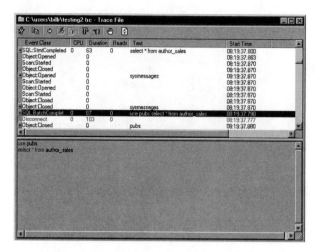

FIGURE 19.5   A Profiler Trace File window.

The Settings option on the Replay menu sets the parameters for execution. On the Replay SQL Server window, shown in Figure 19.6, the most important settings are the synchronization level and replay rate. Synchronization level specifies how to preserve the relationships between events; if you select full synchronization, Profiler will ensure that all previous events have completed before it plays another event.

FIGURE 19.6   Replay settings.

Replay rate sets the rate at which to replay events, and can specify that the player should play them as fast as possible, maintain the interval between events, and maintain the events' relation to the start. The second and last sound similar, but they aren't; just maintaining the interval between events does not mean that they'll occur at the same time they did in previous executions. In this case, an event completing faster than it originally did will move following events up in the schedule, or delay later events if it is slower.

How you use your captured data depends greatly on what it is you're trying to learn. Replays are good for evaluating server loading or speed in satisfying a particular workload. A table containing trace data can be analyzed with SQL when your objective is to fully understand a particular run, or you can use a tool like Excel to do more advanced analysis. When you collect performance data, you should look at what information you are trying to gain, and then collect the data that will support you in your investigation.

If performance is the issue you are trying to address, you can use the Index Tuning Wizard on the Tools menu to analyze your data. With this tool, you specify the database, a trace file (called a workload in the wizard), and the tables to look at, and the wizard will run the trace history and recommend indices to improve performance of the tasks in the trace. After the workload is analyzed, you might choose to have the wizard make the changes for you or save them as SQL in a disk file that you can incorporate into your existing database scripts.

Summary

Profiler provides a valuable service: It allows you to look inside the server while applications (yours or others') are running. You can evaluate the kind and amount of activity for performance reasons, or debug applications by inspecting the SQL they send to the server to verify they are doing what they're supposed to. My experience has been that this simple tool takes a lot of the grunt work out of debugging, and is invaluable for all but the simplest of applications on SQL Server.

For the last chapter, I'm going to introduce you to the Data Transformation Services (DTS), a complicated but valuable addition to the SQL Server toolbox.

LESSON 20

More Powerful Options for Moving Data

This lesson introduces you to one of the best new features of SQL Server: the Data Transformation Services.

If you work in a large organization, or if you are developing database applications, you will need to move data. SQL Server provides several facilities for moving data around, including backups and bcp, a command-line utility, but they only work with SQL Server—you can't use a SQL Server backup to transfer data to an Oracle database. If you can connect to the source and target servers across the network, there is a much better way to move data, both to and from SQL Server or among completely heterogeneous sources.

SQL Server's Data Transformation Services (DTS) can move data between SQL Servers and other database servers directly, with clear graphical interface. With heterogeneous data sources, like moving data from an Oracle 8i server to one on DB2, you can only move table structure and the data in the tables. Between two SQL Server databases, you can also copy the other database objects I've talked about, including indices, stored procedures, constraints, logins, and so forth.

DTS provides much more than just the one-time transfer capability you get from tools like version 6.5's Transfer Manager, or a SELECT ... INTO in Access. With DTS you can create *packages*, predefined setups for transferring and transforming data, that you can then execute at will or schedule to run periodically. This lesson is going to give you a fast tour of the import and export facilities available to you directly from SQL Server Enterprise Manager, but there's much more than I'll be able to show you. If you need to move data constantly or repeatedly among your business's data stores, take a good close look at DTS.

Choosing the Data Source and Destination

In the simplest scenario, DTS moves data and tables between servers. The following steps demonstrate this process.

1. Begin in SQL Server Enterprise Manager. Right-click a SQL Server database that is on one end of the transfer, and choose All Tasks, Import Data or Export Data, depending on whether the database you've chosen is to receive the data or provide it, respectively. This choice only sets the defaults, however, as you will see.

2. Enterprise Manager will display the Import or Export wizard, depending on your choice. Click Next and you will be presented with the Choose a Data Source dialog box; the import version is shown in Figure 20.1.

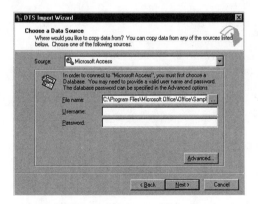

FIGURE 20.1 DTS Import Wizard source selection.

3. You can choose from many different kinds of data sources. In addition to conventional databases like Oracle and Sybase (if you have their client software), you can work with data from dBASE, FoxPro, and Paradox desktop databases, applications like Excel, or any other data source for which you have an ODBC driver. I'll use Access 97 for my example, but you should be able to follow along with most of the supported data sources.

4. In the Import Wizard, you have to give DTS the information it needs to locate and access the source; for a client/server database, you'll need a server name, user ID and password, and for file-based data sources, you'll need the filename and optionally, a user name and password. With ODBC DSNs, the information can vary. For the example, I chose the Microsoft Access source, and then browsed to the Access 97 Northwind database sample. Because there is no security on this database, I left the user name and password blank.

5. Click on the Advanced button in either this dialog or the next, and DTS will show you a list of options you can set on the connection to this data source.

Note With some the list is pretty short (with the Microsoft OLE DB provider for Oracle, for example), and with others it is extensive, as with the Microsoft SQL Server driver. You can ignore things like the Window Handle option, but you might want to set particular properties like the Persist Security Info option, which tells DTS whether to store your user ID and password in the DTS package you're creating.

6. Choose Next after picking the source, and you can specify the destination for the transfer; though you chose to import data to a particular server in the initial step, you can still choose a different one, or a different database on that server. I'll use the pubs database.

7. When you click Next on the destination page of the wizard, you can choose to copy tables, query the source to create the data to transfer, or to transfer objects directly if both ends of the transfer are SQL Server 7.0 databases. Because you're moving between heterogeneous databases, Access 97 and SQL Server 7.0, the last option is grayed out. If you are going to copy data from one or more tables independently, you should choose to copy table(s) from the source, but if you want to assemble data from multiple tables, you should use the query option. For the example, choose to copy tables and click Next.

Tip   Even if you are only copying one table, you can use the query option for transferring. If you do, and you specify the columns in the query from the source in the same order as they are declared in the destination table, they'll be mapped correctly in the transform and you won't have to move them around.

Now comes the fun part. You are presented with a dialog box like the one in Figure 20.2. When first displayed, none of the tables are selected; you can't click Next because you haven't told DTS what data to transfer or where to send it to. On this dialog box, you not only tell it what data to transfer, but more importantly, what to do with the data when moving it.

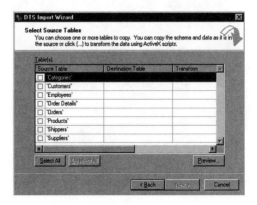

FIGURE 20.2   DTS Import Wizard table selection.

If all you are doing is copying a database from one server to another, probably the most common situation, all you need to do here is select the tables to transfer and click Next. This example will need something more because I'm going to transfer between the Employees table in the Access 97 Northwind sample to the people table you used in the INSERT sample in Lesson 4, "Adding and Changing Data." Because the columns in the two

tables are named differently, I have to tell SQL Server how to transform
the data when it moves it, as follows:

1. Select the check box next to Employees to identify it as the
   source, and then pick the people table as the destination.

2. Click the ellipsis button under the Transform column to see the
   Column Mappings and Transformations dialog box shown in
   Figure 20.3.

3. The choices at the top enable you to create a new table, delete all
   the rows from the destination table before moving the data, or add
   the new rows in with existing data. The last is what I want because
   I already have authors in the table as well that I don't wish to lose.

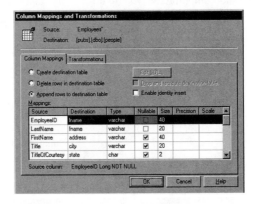

FIGURE 20.3 Mapping the Transform for DTS.

4. Next, you have to set column mappings; that is, you have to tell
   SQL Server which of the columns are equivalent in the two
   tables using the Mappings grid. For each column in the destination table, you have to designate the source column in the other
   table. In the Source column in the grid, the column rows are
   drop-downs, so this is pretty easy. Figure 20.4 shows the dialog
   after setting the mapping to the right columns for the example.

Column mapping This is the process of matching
columns in the source table to those in the destination.

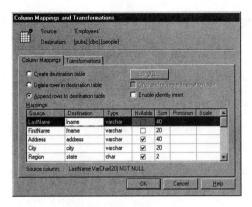

FIGURE 20.4   DTS Mapping with Columns set up.

For any column in the destination table, you can also choose <ignore> if there aren't any values for the column in the source (assuming the column in the destination is nullable or defaulted). To start the transfer, perform the following steps:

1. Click Next. The following page of the wizard allows you to run the script immediately, set up a schedule for running the script periodically, create a package for replication, or a combination of any of these.

2. If you choose to schedule it for later, you must save the package, of course. For demonstration, just run the transform immediately.

3. Click Next again. On the last page of the wizard, you can review the transfer script and then execute it.

A simple, direct transfer like this is good for moving data between servers or databases on one server, when you can move the data as it is. For more complicated operations, you'll need to work with the transfer script.

Transfer Scripts

The Column Mappings and Transformations dialog box also has a Transformations page, shown in Figure 20.5, that you can use to control data transfer more precisely. This facility is key to DTS's power because it allows you not only to vary conversion between columns, but also to completely script what data winds up in the destination. If you don't need to, you can use the default column-by-column copying operation.

With the **Copy the source columns directly to the destination columns** option set, you can click the Advanced button to set options on the copy operation to control how strictly SQL Server interprets data type and size matching. These options are straightforward; you either allow SQL Server to do any conversions necessary, require sizes and types to match exactly, or set custom options for something in between.

Selecting **Transform information as it is copied to the destination** activates the script box in the bottom half of the dialog. DTS writes a starter script in this box for you that copies columns directly, but you are free to edit this as you wish. The illustration shows the script that DTS created to map the columns as I showed before.

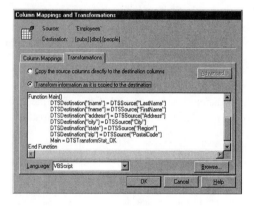

FIGURE 20.5   DTS Transformation Script.

The script you write for the transformation can be as complicated as you need it to be, and can either be VBScript or JScript, based on the Language selection on the dialog. DTS will execute the script for every row in the source table, by default. You use the DTSSource and DTSDestination objects, which represent the current row in the source data and the row that will be created in the destination, to create destination rows from the source data. The simple copy operation demonstrated in Figure 20.5 copies data from DTSSource to DTSDestination, but you can also combine columns, break them up, calculate destination columns from values in the source, or whatever your need indicates.

You control the results of the script by assigning a value to return to DTS when the script completes. Usually the value you return will be either DTSTransformStat_OK to tell DTS to create the new row in the destination database (as in the example), or DTSTransformStat_SkipRow, to tell DTS to drop the current source row and move on to the next one without creating a row in the destination table. You might use your script to validate data from the source, for example, and skip those rows that didn't make the grade. You return the value to DTS by assigning it to the name of the script function, as in the last statement of the example.

When you've finished editing a script, clicking **OK** returns you to the source tables, where you can select other tables and set them up if necessary.

For More Information About DTS

In this lesson, I've shown you the Import Wizard of DTS. A capable tool on its own, it is only a small part of the function DTS provides you. I skipped discussion of replication and the Microsoft Repository intentionally, for example, because the discussion they require just wouldn't fit in the book. I've had to make such decisions in most of the topics I've covered, but it's particularly difficult for a feature as powerful as DTS.

You can use DTS to create data marts in strategic locations; unlike replication, usually used for those scenarios, you can set up filters and massage the data in a single tool to create customized data solutions on your distributed servers. In the other direction, DTS and the Repository can be used to assemble data into a data warehouse, scrubbing the information as it is acquired, and tracking its origin and succeeding steps through your data infrastructure. With its combination of transformation, scheduling, and accounting, I expect this will be one of the most useful technologies in SQL Server 7.

It should come as no surprise that there is a lot more information on DTS in the SQL Server documentation. DTS itself has its own book in the root of Books Online, titled, logically, *Data Transformation Services*. In particular, this reference goes into much more detail on creating warehouse applications with DTS, using the DTS Designer to lay out data connections and flows, execute programs and scripts, and other tasks required in your data architecture. If you need to build more potent data transfers than the simple source-to-destination transfer I've shown you, look here.

To create your own DTS-based applications, you should turn to the "DTS Programming" topic under *Building SQL Server Applications*. Here you will find information on using the DTS COM objects from applications you write. Because DTS is exposed to the world through objects, just like the ADO objects you used in ASP, you can write client applications using C++, Visual Basic, or any other COM-aware environment; you can even put a Web interface on DTS with ASP!

Summary

It seems I've reached the conclusion, not for the lesson, this time, but for the book. In this lesson, I've given you a glimpse into the powerful data transfer and transformation capability in the SQL Server Data Transformation Services, and a couple of pointers into other books for more information. If you will be doing any development work with databases, even if you only need to get data into your desktop from a company database, you'll find DTS a powerful, but easy-to-use, tool for the job.

I hope you found both the book and SQL Server useful. I've shown you what you need to get off and running in SQL Server, and if you've gone through all the lessons, you've gained a very good start in your work with a very good database. Far more than a simple data store, SQL Server 7 provides a data and processing environment with a broad enough set of capabilities to meet many needs out of the box. For those needs it doesn't address immediately, you've learned several ways to add value with other tools.

If you continue working with SQL Server, you'll keep learning. I wish you well in your journey, and I hope it is as enjoyable as mine has been.

INDEX

F

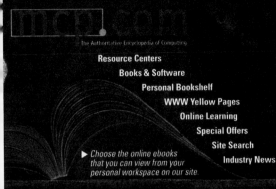

Other Related Titles

Microsoft SQL Server 7.0 DBA Survival Guide
Mark Spenik and Orryn Sledge
ISBN: 0-672-31226-3
$49.99 USA/$71.95 CAN

Sams Teach Yourself Microsoft Access 2000 in 10 Minutes
Faithe Wempen
ISBN: 0-672-31487-8
$12.99 USA/$19.95 CAN

Microsoft SQL Server 7.0 Programming Unleashed
John Papa, et al.
ISBN: 0-672-31293-X
$49.99 USA/$74.95 CAN

Microsoft SQL Server 7.0 Unleashed
Sharon Bjeletich, Greg Mable et al.
ISBN: 0-672-31227-1
$49.99 USA/$71.95 CAN

Windows NT 4 Server Unleashed, Second Edition
Jason Garms
ISBN: 0-672-31249-2
$49.99 USA/$74.95 CAN

Sams Teach Yourself Visual Basic 6 in 10 Minutes
Lowell Mauer, et al.
ISBN: 0-672-31458-4
$12.99 USA/$18.95 CAN

Programming Windows 98/NT Unleashed
Viktor Toth
ISBN: 0-672-31353-7
$49.99 USA/$71.95 CAN

Microsoft Access 2000 Development Unleashed
Forte, Howe, and Ralston
ISBN: 0-672-31291-3
$39.99 USA/$59.95 CAN

Visual InterDev 6 Unleashed
Paul Thurrott, et al.
ISBN: 0-672-31262-X
$49.99 USA/$74.95 CAN

Sams Teach Yourself Microsoft SQL Server 7.0 in 21 Days
Richard Waymire and Rick Sawtell
ISBN: 0-672-31290-5
$39.99 USA/$57.95 CAN

SAMS

www.samspublishing.com

Sams Teach Yourself Windows NT Server 4 in 14 Days
Peter Davis
ISBN: 0-672-31019-8
$35.00 USA/$50.95 CAN

All prices are subject to change.